"In THE THUNDER POET Steve takes you on a trip to the most remote and darkest places on the African continent. You will accompany him on an excursion to where darkness meets light. If you journey with him, you will not be bored. I, for one, was changed forever!"

Ron Buck President, Asset Management
Nashville, Tennessee

"Through poetic prose, Steve Taylor unfurls some of the most cherished Scripture that we thought we already understood."

Judy Hart, Sunday School Teacher
and Retired English Professor

"Are you ready for an adventure with God and a life that is more bold and brave than you could ever imagine? THE THUNDER POET is the place to start."

Matthew Gaither, Internet Salesperson Manager and Blogger—**Matthew515.com**

THE
THUNDER POET

Rhyming Life with God's
Indigenous Design

Steven R. Taylor

blood washed khaki publishing

Copyright

©2018 Steven R. Taylor

All rights reserved. No part of this book may be used or reproduced by any means, graphic, electronic, or mechanical, including photocopying, recording, taping or by any information storage retrieval system without the written permission of the publisher except in the case of quotations embodied in critical articles and reviews.

All Scripture quotes are from the Holman Christian Standard Version of the Bible, 1999, 2000, 2002, 2003 by Holman Bible Publisher, Nashville, Tennessee, unless otherwise noted.

ISBN: 978-0-9887261-4-7 Paperback
ISBN: 978-0-9887261-5-4 Kindle

Blood Washed Khaki Publishing
409 N. Main Street, Pratt, Kansas 67124
Printed in the United States of America
www.bloodwashedkhaki.com

Cover Design: Main Focus Photography, using photo images from Mike Blair of Mike Blair Outdoors for (the Lightning), and Steve Taylor for (the Elephant).

Edited by: Judy Hart

DEDICATION

For Shirley—my love and faithful companion. Thank you for being my lifetime partner as we've shared these many years of adventure. Thank you for your support, patience, and forgiveness. Thank you most of all for your sacrificial love—a love that flows from the purity of your heart. You have brought balance to the meter of a life-poem that the Poet still edits today. *"Blessed are the pure in heart for they shall see God."* (Matthew 5:8)

ACKNOWLEDGEMENTS

I wish to express my deepest gratitude and profound admiration for the following people who in an amazingly broad diversity of ways have inspired and participated in the production of this book.

Judy Hart, retired English Professor, one of the most deeply committed Christians I've ever known, and one of the best editors in America — for her gifted and sensitive editorial work and literary encouragement.

Mike Blair, outdoor photographer and filmmaker — for his contribution of the lightning photo image essential to the design of the cover. (mikeblairoutdoors.com)

Buck DeVries, lion hunter, conservationist, deep personal friend — for being the embodiment of everything I love about wild Africa, and for his wife Martie and his family's support of our ministry over the years.

The International Mission Board of the Southern Baptist Convention — for making it possible for us to spend those initial years in Africa, and for being the best and most complete support base missionaries could ever hope for.

The BaTonga people of the Zambezi River Valley — Because of their lives, my life will never be the same. Thank you for including me, and for interrupting Tonga history so I could get on board and become a part of it.

First Southern Baptist Church, Pratt, Kansas, as well as other faithful churches with whom I've been associated — for supporting and making possible each year a return to the Zambezi River Valley for a short-term mission trip with a wonderful group of volunteers, and for allowing time and opportunity for the preparation of Biblical messages from God's Word.

My children, Purity, Rye, and McKelvey, all who love the Lord, missions, adventure, and the African people — for being living testimonies of the impact of legacy, each having played significant roles in the various stories of this volume, and each who are living out the adventure of a poetic rhyme in the different areas and roles to which they have been called throughout the world.

CONTENTS

Dedication

Acknowledgements

Foreword

Introduction: A life That Rhymes   1

1. Creation's Testament   9

2. The Voice of the Wilderness   23

3. Snake Stories   39

4. The Sapient Safari   65

5. Plagiarized Poems and Passionless Lives   101

6. Nesting in a Shadow   119

7. A Log Left Burning in an African Campfire   145

8. Finding Rhyme on the Other Side Of Fear   169

About the Author   207

Notes   209

Preview of Steve's Previous Book   223

FOREWORD

I'm a Christian. So, what does it mean to say, "I'm a Christian?" Or maybe a better question to ask is, "What should it mean to be a Christian?" Being a Christian means many things to people. There are some who believe being a Christian means you believe God exists, that you even believe Jesus died on the cross to forgive sin, and that you are fairly certain that you believe Jesus resurrected three days after being crucified.

Others believe being a Christian means you are doing your best to be a good person. These people are convinced your life is like a set of balance scales. The day will come when you will stand before God and He will weigh-out the good and the bad of your life. If the good of your life is more abundant than the bad, you get to go to Heaven. But if the bad of your life is greater than the good, you are doomed to a place called Hell. Of course, most people who believe like this are quick to compare their lives to the lives of others. They are sure their life is filled with more good than bad. And they are certain they live better than most people they know. So, their chance of making it to Heaven is pretty good.

Let me be as clear as I can be. These two examples of what people believe makes them a Christian are both wrong. If you fit into the group who believes the things stated above, you are not a Christian.

To be a Christian means you are a follower of Christ. You have acknowledged you are a sinner. It is a fact for you that you understand there is no reason God should save you and take you to Heaven. By faith you have realized Jesus died on the cross for your sin. By faith you have accepted as fact He rose from the dead. And you have repented of your sin and totally given your life to Christ. You are a Christ-follower. You believe His word, not only, can guide your life. But you are allowing His word to guide your life.

Now, we have settled the truth concerning what it means to be a Christian there is another question we must answer. This question is a life changing question. The personal answer you give for this question will be seen in your life every day. Here it is—the question of the day. Are you a growing Christian?

Some will answer this challenging question with a definite, "Yes." Others will answer this question with words like, "I certainly want to grow in my faith." I am of the opinion every Christian grows. If you are a Christian, you are growing, and you desire to grow more and more.

My friend, Steve Taylor, has written this book with you in mind. THE THUNDER POET is a book for serious believers. You will learn much about your walk in the Lord and what your walk will look like as you grow in Christ.

I have known Steve Taylor, personally, for several years. I have known him by reputation and through mutual friends for many years. Steve has served as a pastor, a teacher, and a deep bush missionary in Southern Africa.

There are a lot of things I like about Steve Taylor, one of which is no one can tell a story better than Steve. I have sat for hours and have listened to him speak of his ministry in the deep bush of Africa. He can thrill your mind with the stories of lions, elephants and snakes. He can thrill your soul with accounts of individuals and entire villages coming to Christ under his ministry.

THE THUNDER POET is a book of stories and spiritual truth. It is a book filled with understanding concerning the Christian walk. Every story in this volume is well written, but more than being well written, every story will teach you gospel truth.

Steve Taylor writes with "sizzle". His words will paint amazing pictures of the bush in Africa. You will think you are in the jeep with him as you travel over roads lined with explosive devices which remain in war-torn nations. As you travel with Steve to take the gospel to people many will never see you will enjoy his amazing teaching. He will teach academic facts and turn them into incredible spiritual truths.

THE THUNDER POET will stretch your mind and your heart. There will be many times, as you read this material, you will exclaim out loud, "I did not know that." Perhaps you will be anxious to say to others, "Did you know..." But more than the knowledge you will gain you are about to improve your walk with the Lord.

I'm thrilled you are reading Steve's book. I'm sure you will join me, as you read, in growing in the Lord. You are about to experience the bush of Africa in a way like never before. You will be changed for your good and glory of our God.

Enjoy, THE THUNDER POET!

Dr. Ted Kersh,
Bible Teacher, Equipped By His Word

Introduction

A Life That Rhymes

"O for a voice like thunder, and a tongue to drown the throat of war!"
William Blake[1]

    The sky was dark and stagnant—inky black with glints of starlight peeking through it like sparkling drool in the gaping mouth of a testy territorial mamba. Pasty grey clouds hung in its corners as thick as the tacky ashen wallow silt that clings to the back of a mud-caked buffalo. Silence dominated the darkness—that eerie silence that comes when the killing is finished and the predators of the bush have had their fill—that weighty hushed silence you feel between the beats of your heart when an elephant treads too closely to your tent in the middle of the night.
    Just before daybreak a gentle breeze stirred, swelling in the distance at first, then lightly caressing the face of the flat Zambezi like the soothing black hand of a loving Tonga mother brushing away flies from the grimacing eyes of her fevered child. The King

of Light breathed out a pleasured sigh as He calmed His anxious creatures. He fanned away their fear by scattering the gloom of an ominous sky and simultaneously releasing the tether that held back His predatory dawn.

Rising with the speed of a sprinting cheetah and riding low on the sinuous back of a spinning shadow, an ever alert champion positioned himself, firmly planting his sunlit claws, preparing for the pounce. Crouching carefully beneath the concealment of a soon to be discarded cloak and hastening with a pace that outstripped the tempo of his fiery heart, daybreak leapt, knocking the legs from beneath the darkness in mid-stride.

The attack was sudden and thorough. A single slash across the throat of the horizon was all it took. A luminous pool of back-lit gore bled out in the east, reddening a pallid backdrop with crimson vitality. Scattered rag-like clouds formed useless tourniquets. They could do nothing to stop the bleeding. Leftover vestiges from a pre-dawn storm, these tattered sky-bandages were simply outmatched. They swiftly became glowing filaments—converted conductors of sorts, reflecting the radiance of a determined pursuer they desperately tried to restrain.

The Predacious Night-Conqueror was none other than the Divine Creator Himself—the Sworn Imperial Enemy of Darkness. He had imagined the beginning of a new day and the mere thought of His artistry had accomplished its purpose. Another one of His poetic masterpieces was underway and there was no holding it back.

The Thunder Poet

Eastward in the distance, I heard the low muffled growl of the Maker's voice rumbling across the skyline, proudly proclaiming the success of another daybreak, and adding final commentary to the completion of His task. With that, the great Thunder Poet wrote the last line of His morning sonnet, beginning His day with a newly scribbled song of dawn, concurrently composing a new set of opportunities for the up and about, while liberating cringing captives from their fear of darkness and the night.

The great God of Heaven was at it again, and as usual, I had a front row seat. I had begun my day as I often did then, watching a sunrise, pondering the magnitude of God's poetic expression, standing in the midst of majesty on the banks of the Zambezi River.

The Perfect Poet

Robert Browning once called God, "the perfect Poet."[2] That is how the Bible portrays Him, too. With thoughts as bold and dazzling as lightning and a voice as impressive and resounding as thunder, He pours out His poetry across the entirety of His creation and into the life of every listening believer.

The Greek word *poiema* is used only twice in the New Testament, once in Romans 1:20 and once in Ephesians 2:10, and each time it is used, it is translated in our English versions as *"creation,"* *"workmanship,"* or *"what He has made."* From the word *poiema*—the thing created—we get our English word poem. *Poiema* reminds us that whatever God creates, He creates as a poetic masterpiece. This is true of His creation of the natural world, and it is also true of His creative purpose of redemption for our individual lives.

In fact, Scripture reveals that God has produced two great poetic masterpieces—creation and redemption. Thus the interrelated doctrines of His design and of His deliverance can never be separated. Bible passages like John 1:1-14, Colossians 1:16-19, and Hebrews 1:1-3 teach us whatever is revealed in Scripture about the nature of our Creator also instructs us about the nature of our Savior. The great "Thunder Poet," the Creator-Savior, is none other than the Lord Jesus Christ, our Maker and Redeemer. The Bible tells us that we are therefore to *"worship the Maker of heaven and earth . . . ."* (Revelation 14:7)

We Are God's Poems

According to Ephesians 2:10, *"We are His creation (poemia), created in Christ Jesus for good works, which God prepared ahead of time so we should walk in them."* Every person's life is intended to be a spectacular poetic saga, composed in the mind of God and inscribed on a tiny page called time, a product of the Poet's ingenuity, a statement of His creative artistry, and an articulation of His superb thought, yet the reality of a fulfilled life comes only when life is lived in response to God's intended plan.

The Thunder Poet

The Poet's Autobiography

Having no other source from which to create authentic life, God began our lives by chiseling a reflection from His own personal mirror, thus creating man in His image and giving us the privilege of living out that image in this world. Therefore, life rightly lived in response to and in harmony with God's intended purpose is the fulfillment of the Father's poetic plan. Life, correctly lived rhymes with God's indigenous design, that being a reflection of His image in this world.

Yevgeny Yevtushenko once said, "A poet's autobiography is his poetry. Anything else is just a footnote."[3] What is true about earthly poets is also true about the Almighty. Could this be why human beings are never satisfied with life apart from the fulfillment of their destinies in Christ? Have we missed the awesome privilege that has been offered to us through redemption? We are invited to be "autobiographies" of the Most High; living in this world, resonating His reality and speaking His truth to mankind. We are called to be agents of His character, writers of His answer, and speakers of His truth, reflectors of the image of His Son, yet too often we have settled instead for merely being cultural "footnotes" of a society that has lost its way.

James Hastings describes the process like this, "The poem depends entirely on the poet for its creation. It is the unveiling of the deepest and most intimate secrecies of his heart. His own image is projected over every page, and it is this poignant personal element in poetry that makes it so beautiful. Men are God's poems. The intimacies of God's heart are expressed in man—God's highest thoughts, God's deepest emotions. When a man is finished at last in the likeness of Christ, God's sense of beauty is satisfied in Him."4

Antiphons

When it comes to any serious discussion of poetry, especially when it comes to a consideration of its vital sound, rhyme and meter play significant roles. These functions are specifically true in the case of English poetry.

By contrast, "the chief device of Biblical poetry in ancient Hebrew was parallelism, a rhetorical structure in which successive lines reflected each other. Hebrew poetry was a verse form that lent itself to antiphonal, or call and response performance."5 During an antiphonal performance, a singer or group of singers would respond, echoing the sound of the first. This call and response pattern is typical of the kind of life we should live in response to the call of Christ in our own lives. In fact, our lives, as poems of God, have much in common with this ancient Biblical poetic form. According to the teachings of Scripture, our lives are meant to be antiphons, rhyming with the poetic intention of the Father's heart. Life lived at its maximized potential is life lived in harmony with God's original composition and congruent with His initial design. Only when we begin to live in this way, can we grasp what Jesus was saying in John 10:10

The Thunder Poet

when He said that the very reason for His coming was so we could have *"life and have it in abundance."*

When Christ speaks, we believers, like all livings things, should respond with what we describe as "our lives." But in order to live "our lives" to their fullest, we must understand that they are not "our" lives at all. We are His "*workmanship.*" We are His "animated poetry." We are His expressive poem. It is in Him that *"we live and move and have our being."* (Acts 17:28)

In her book, A PLACE OF HEALING, Joni Eareckson Tada, who became a quadriplegic after a tragic diving accident as a young person, refers to this concept of life as God's poetry. "God has a plan and purpose for my time on earth. He is the master artist and sculptor, and He is the One Who chooses the tools He will use to perfect His workmanship. . . . Am I to tell Him which tools He can use and which tools He can't use in the lifelong task of perfecting me and molding me into the beautiful image of Jesus? Do I really know better than Him, so that I can state without equivocation that it's always His will to heal me of every physical affliction? If I am His poem, do I have the right to say, 'No Lord. You need to trim line number two and brighten up lines three and five. They're just a little bit dark.' Do I, the poem, the thing being written, know more than the poet?"[6]

Our lives are His poetry. This book is about rhyming life with God's indigenous design and discovering maximized living by becoming the personal expressive poem God intended for each of us to be. It is about being conformed to the image of

Christ and rejecting the temptation to become a "footnote" of this world. It is a book about destiny—about finding and living out God's unique objective and making the most of every moment of life. This is consistent with the great Thunder Poet's original plan. It is His premeditated purpose. This is what He *"prepared ahead of time"* for us to do.

Chapter 1

Creation's Testament

"The Creator has gifted the whole universe with language, but few are the hearts that can interpret it."
Edward Bulwer Lytton[1]

The yellow wedge of a vivid half-moon ascended on the rim of a smoke-veiled late September African night sky. It rose quickly, yet smoothly, like a lemon slice buoyed by bubbles in a glass of carbonated cola. The pungent biting scent of smoldering seasonal bush fires dominated my senses. As I switched off the lantern inside my Wolfskin tent, someplace in the distance a lonely hyena found his voice and his haunting howl pierced the silent darkness of the wee hours. Just outside my tent in a pale blue hue of muted lunar light, a small dark insect cast a sturdy shadow that fell across the powder-fine grit of a Kalahari sand pathway. Remarkably, this diminutive little creature makes its way in a perfectly straight line on the forest floor of the Zambezi River Valley. And it accomplishes that feat with the dexterity of an acrobat, while standing on its front legs, walking backwards, and hauling a treasure of filth fifty times the weight of its own body.

The African dung-ball-rolling beetle is one of Africa's most common, yet least known or understood creatures. Though relatives of this little beetle come in more than 37,000 varieties worldwide, and even though they are found on every continent except Antarctica, this particular variety is one of the most intriguingly underrated symbols of the African wild. Perhaps the most amazing fact about this tiny creature is that he transports his plunder following a straight line toward his nest regardless of obstacles, and the incredible reason he is able to do this undeterred is because he navigates his journey by using the light of the moon and stars.

According to recent research done by Dr. Marie Dacke, a South African entomologist who has spent years studying the behavior of African dung-ball-rolling beetles, these tiny insects use the sun, the moon, and even celestial polarization to move along on a straight path. In fact, her findings provide the first documented evidence for use of the Milky Way for orientation by any creature in the animal kingdom. Dung beetles actually use the Milky Way like ancient sailors used a compass and sextant. Currently, Dr. Dacke is investigating a strange little dance that these small creatures do on top of their ball of poop. Her hypothesis is that this behavior marks the precise moment the little beetle takes its bearings.[2]

Is that not remarkable? It is as if God has gone to extraordinary lengths just to get our attention and to convince us of His presence in the midst of the world's denial of His creative poetry.

"Validation Poetry"

Unfortunately, most people who visit Africa miss the magic of the moment that I describe above simply because they get so caught up in running here and there, viewing elephants, lions, rhino, and other "glamorous" game of the bush. They never discover that these petite little dung beetles even exist. The average tourist reasons, "Even if they do exist, what would be the purpose for giving these tiny creatures any consideration or second thought?" But, as anyone who has spent much time in Africa knows, observation of these little insects as they go through their daily routine near wild game watering holes is one of the most common sights in the African bush.

Only lately have we realized what makes these beetles so special is the relatively recent scientific discovery concerning their reliance on celestial cues from the galaxy and that they actually use the Milky Way like we use a GPS. The fact that they behave in such a way is a resounding shout of testimony to the presence and involvement of the Creator in their lives. It is as if the Almighty, Himself, is calling out, *"I'm here! I'm present! Just when you think there is a creature so lowly that I am not engaged in his life or when you think there is a creature so crude that I would not care to be so involved with him, the behavior of these humble little creatures is a testimony to My design."*

So using the unique characteristics of the dung beetle, God actually contrives a new category of poetry—"validation poetry." The lyrical lines in the life of a dung beetle vividly portray the reality and involvement of God in His creative process. These storylines clearly verify and validate God's presence. In fact, all of creation shouts confirmation of His testimony.

Years ago, Johannes Kepler, the father of modern astronomy said, "The undevout astronomer is a mad man."[3] That was Kepler's way of saying God's presence and involvement in His creation is so obvious that only a fool or determined rejecter of reality could possibly deny that truth.

Perhaps that is why the secular worldview is in direct opposition to a Creator, why naturalism at its core is atheistic, and why the thrust of the evolutionary theory is an attempt to tell the story of our origins without God. Perhaps that is also why any serious consideration of the evolutionary hypothesis always leaves a thinking person with a suspicion of the theory's incredible claims when it comes to an attempt to explain the origin of life apart from the existence and involvement of God. The illogical mental contortions required by a position that tries to explain the origin of life without the existence of God are ludicrous. Someone described it like trying to dive for sand dollars in the ocean while holding a beach ball in your arms. The ball always rushes to the surface, and it requires considerable effort to keep it in your arms under the water. The same is true with an effort to deny the reality of God from an observation of

The Thunder Poet

creation. That position requires deliberate intent and denial. With any serious observation of the natural world, the truth of God's existence just keeps coming to the surface, again and again.

Wherever we travel in the world we find people asking questions about God. They want to know whether or not God exists. Why do you think that comes up so often? Could it be that the world is made in such a way that people naturally see a connection between the creation and a Creator? The creation, itself, tells us something about God. John Calvin said, "Men cannot open their eyes without being compelled to see Him . . . there is not a spot in the universe wherein you cannot discern at least some sparks of His glory."[4]

Have you ever noticed that some artists have such a distinct style in their artistic expression that every time you see a work by that particular artist you can immediately detect who is the painter simply by looking at the style? It is that way with the abstract cubism of Picasso and also that way with the bizarre images like melting clocks and elephants reflecting images of swans in the works of Salvador Dali. The style of the artist is clearly seen in his artistic design.

I've noticed this characteristic even in the truly great contemporary artists, too. Prior to the years that my family and I lived in Africa, as well as in the years following, we lived for many years in New Mexico. There I had the privilege to observe a lot of western and Native American art. Over the years I became acquainted with the works of some of the truly great western artists. After a while it becomes relatively easy to spot and identify the works of artists like R. C. Gorman, who has been called "the Picasso of Native American art," or the gorgeous black pottery of Maria Martinez. One of my favorite western artists is a man named Howard Terpning. Terpning's American Indian subjects are always distinguishable simply by the chiseled, rugged features of his style. While I am not an art critic, nor am I a trained appraiser, the style of Terpning's work is so distinctive that I can identify them immediately whenever I see an example of his art.

The same is true with the Thunder Poet. The wonder and beauty of the natural world points to a Creator Who is imaginative, personal, stunning, and artistic. The characteristics of His "style" are evident. Everywhere He shouts through His creation, *"I'm here! I'm here!"*

"Hey You Guys, I'm Over Here!"

One of my all-time favorite comedy films is entitled *The Three Amigos* starring the talented comedians, Steve Martin, Chevy Chase, and Martin Short. The film is about a team of turn-of-the-century starving "cowboy actors" who get involved with rescuing a town of peasants south of the border, who are being held under the oppression of a bad outlaw named El Juapo. At the beginning of the film, Martin, Chase, and Short have to break into the movie studios to retrieve their official *Amigo* outfits. In an attempt to remain concealed and clandestine, Steve Martin takes the lead and positions himself on top of the studio building while his "amigos" remain crouched inconspicuously on the far side of the lot. In an effort to get the attention of Chase and Short, Steve Martin begins with a light, cautious voice, making unassertive bird calls. These calls go completely unnoticed by the two fellow "amigos" hunkered on the ground. Martin decides he must increase his volume, so he proceeds to make louder calls like those of coyotes and ravens, but still his calls go undetected. Finally, after a series of attempts, he shouts in desperation at the top of his voice with a very obvious appeal, *"Hey, you guys, I'm over here!"* With that, the two remaining "amigos" finally get the message and the action of the storyline in the film begins.[5]

I think that is how God must sometimes feel about us. He sends message after message through His creation, but we tend to be incredibly slow to "get it." So, with evidence as obvious as dung beetles who navigate their journeys using the Milky Way, He shouts at the top of His voice from heaven, *"Hey, you guys, I'm over here."*

The Indigenous Language of God

In Romans 1:20, the Apostle Paul tells us that when God first communicates with man, He speaks in a dialect called "creation." Before there were Scriptures and before God spoke to the patriarchs and to Moses as a man would speak to his friend, the Creator conversed through His creation. The Bible portrays His communication through nature as God's <u>indigenous language</u>. It is His "creation language" that expresses God's original uninhibited contact. In fact, such language is the medium God chose for a primary and effective presentation of the essence of Who He is. He still speaks through His creation today.

Paul expresses God's initial communication like this, *"From the creation of the world His invisible attributes, that is, His eternal power and divine nature, have been <u>clearly seen</u>, being understood through <u>what He has made</u> (poemia). As a result, people are without excuse." (*Romans 1:20 *emphasis mine*) With that statement Paul is affirming what has already been asserted in one of the greatest Psalms in Scripture. *"The heavens declare the glory of God, and the sky proclaims the work of His hands. Day after day they pour out speech; night after night they communicate knowledge. There is no speech; there are no words; their voice is not heard. Their message has gone out to all the earth, and their words to the ends of the inhabited world."* (Psalm 19:1-4)

These passages depict what theologians describe as "general revelation," and it is this revelation through creation that God uses to first make Himself known to man. Mike Mason describes this concept powerfully. "Nature still stands as [God's] first and sufficient revelation, His first gospel. Mother nature is theology's subconscious. She is our Father's mother tongue."[6]

The Heavens Communicate Knowledge

The essence of Mason's description is why David says, *"The heavens declare the glory of God,*

The Thunder Poet

and the sky proclaims the work of His hands. Day after day they pour out speech; night after night they communicate knowledge."

I am convinced that every parent should have at least a rudimentary understanding of astronomy. I think we should be able to go out and show our children or grandchildren the glory of God in the stars. In fact, I believe a basic grasp of astronomy is a significant part of our witness for Christ. If the heavens declare the glory of God, we should find ways to point that out.

Each year in Zimbabwe during our Rock Cry Expedition, I spend at least a portion of one of the team's deep bush camping nights pointing out various things about the stars in the Southern Hemisphere. Some of the things I share involve navigation principles and the location of constellations that are unique to viewing from that part of the world. Yet, other things I share with the group simply relate to celestial facts that bring glory to God.

For example, in the constellation Orion there is a star called Betelgeuse. Betelgeuse is one of the largest known stars. It is a red supergiant, perhaps better defined as a hypergiant. Betelgeuse is 100,000 times brighter than our sun, and it is located at the point of the right shoulder of Orion.

The most amazing fact about Betelgeuse relates not to its location, but rather to its size. It is so large that it is actually twice the size of the earth's orbit around the sun. That's a diameter of 600 million miles. Yet even at that enormous size, it still takes the light from Betelgeuse 640 light years to reach our earth. And there are billions and billions of stars beyond that. Perhaps the vast magnitude and immense distance is why the psalmist says, *"The heavens declare the glory of God."*

What kind of incredible creative energy does it take to make a universe like this? GOD'S KIND! In fact, Colossians 1:16 says, *"All things were created through Him and for Him."* Every created thing exists for the purpose of glorifying Him.

The psalmist tells us that the measureless universe exists for that purpose. The universe is indescribably massive. Our "home" galaxy is called the Milky Way and it is only a tiny part of the universe, yet it contains between 100 and 400 billion stars. And that's just one galaxy. Do you have any idea how many galaxies there are?

In 1995, scientists picked out a little section of the night sky that was unusually devoid of stars. To the naked eye, and even in a normal telescope, this region looked empty and black, and the section was tiny compared to the known universe. In fact, it covered the same amount of sky that a tennis ball would cover if you pitched it 100 yards above you and then froze it there. Those scientists used the Hubble Telescope to take a 10-day long exposure of the empty region to find out what was out there deep in the blackness. They came back with this: over 10,000 tiny dots of light. But as they began to examine the photo closely, they discovered that those tiny dots of light were not stars. They were galaxies. And each one of those galaxies contains around 100 billion stars. Keep in mind that this was all photographed in a pinpoint-

The Thunder Poet

sized square of the night sky. Scientists used the information from this photo to postulate that the observable universe contains over 100 billion galaxies, and each one of those galaxies contains 100-400 billion stars. That puts the total number of stars in the observable universe at around 100 sextillion stars. How many is that? To put that in perspective, people at the University of Hawaii spent an unreasonable amount of time calculating an estimate for the number of grains of sand in the world. That includes the number of grains of sands on the beaches of Hawaii as well as the number of grains of sand on every other beach in the world, plus all the sand not found on beaches. They came up with the number 7.5 quintillion. What that means is that for every grain of sand there is on Earth, there are about 10,000 stars in the universe.[7] No wonder the psalmist said, *"The heavens declare the glory of God."*

"Then Comes a Roaring"

In the Bible there is an obvious connection between creation and communication, and because of this connection, whenever the sound of the Lord's voice is described in Scripture, images of nature are most often utilized as the way of describing it. No sound articulated by mere man is sufficient to convey an adequate simile. An element from the natural world seems needed to give God's voice ample description.

The prophets Hosea and Amos refer to God's voice like that of a roaring lion. (Hosea 11:10, Amos

3:8) The book of Revelation depicts it like the sound of a giant waterfall (1:15). The prophet Ezekiel reiterates that description, (43:2) but adds that it sounds like something similar to a wilderness stampede (3:12). Scripture asserts repeatedly that whenever the Almighty speaks, His accent reverberates with the sounds of vast wild places, His rhetoric is untamed, and His tonal inflection rings with the resonance of the singing stars. His creation and His communication are inseparable. In fact, wherever we find the creation story portrayed in the Bible, it is His Word that is the medium of creation, not His Hands.

This feature is so characteristic in the Old Testament book of Job that the book cannot be understood apart from recognizing that when the Almighty communicates, He speaks with the vocabulary of a Creator through the vernacular of creation. In fact, in Job, the sound and force of God's voice are described in many ways, but the metaphorical images most often used are associated with wild or natural things. Employed are the voices and actions of wild animals, the songs of the birds, the intricacies of the insects and the fish of the sea, the natural phenomena of the weather patterns, and the mysteries of the cosmos—all representative voices of creation.

Yet noticeably, the most explicit description of God's voice found in Job's book depicts His voice as sounding like thunder. *"My heart pounds at this and leaps from my chest. Just listen to His <u>thunderous</u> voice and the rumbling that comes from His mouth.*

The Thunder Poet

He lets it loose beneath the entire sky; His lightning to the ends of the earth. <u>Then</u> there <u>comes a roaring</u> sound; God <u>thunders</u> with His majestic voice. He does not restrain the lightning when His rumbling voice is heard. God <u>thunders</u> marvelously with His voice; He does great things that we cannot comprehend" (Job 37:1-5, emphasis mine*).*

In God's Word no sound more than the sound of thunder accurately conveys the regal, breathtaking voice of God. Possibly that is why when the Father affirms the Son in John 12:29, and the people heard His voice, some said *"it thundered."* Thunder is the pinnacle depiction of His vocal communication. It sufficiently embodies the whole cacophony of the Creator's voice. And that is why the Bible so often links His voice with the piercingly strident sound of thunder. While human beings were created in the image of God's Person, it seems a natural inference that thunder was created in the image of His voice (Exodus 19:19, 1 Samuel 2:10, 7:10, 2 Samuel 22:14, Job 40:9, Psalm 18:13, 29:3, 69:33, 81:7, 104:7, John 12:29, Revelation 14:2). The Poet of Heaven is the great <u>Thunder Poet</u>. When He speaks, He speaks with the voice of creation. When He speaks, He speaks with a voice of thunder. This is the testament of creation.

Chapter 2

The Voice of the Wilderness

"Some people talk to animals. Not many listen though. That is the problem."
Alan A. Milne – Winnie the Pooh[1]

Creation's testament is plainly seen and clearly heard in the context of the wilderness. Wilderness is another word for the natural world that surrounds us, including the whole environment and all animal life. The United States federal government defines wilderness as "an area that appears to be affected primarily by the forces of nature, with the imprint of human influence essentially unnoticeable . . . areas untrammeled by man."[2]

Wilderness is a major topic throughout Scripture. A number of Hebrew and Greek words in the Bible are translated as "wilderness." These combined are mentioned 245 times in the Old Testament and 35 times in the New. The wilderness is the setting for much of God's revelation of Himself, for His call of those He significantly uses, and for the fashioning of their lives.

Generally speaking, we are city dwellers and our tendency is to avoid the wilderness unless we determine there is something to be gained from a visit. But in Scripture, the wilderness is an essential part of God's story. Some of the most important things that happen in the Bible happen in wild places—everything from man's creation to the initiation of Christ's public ministry, to the preparation of Moses, to the equipping of David, to the restoration of Elijah, and to the training of the Apostle Paul. Many of the most transformative moments in Christ's ministry occurred in remote locations, and Jesus, more than anyone else in Scripture, made it His practice to return to the wild solitary places whenever He needed to be refreshed and revitalized.[3]

In Scripture, the wilderness is an environmental crucible, a place of testing, a place for encountering God, and a place of deep spiritual preparation and clarification. God speaks distinctly in the context of it. Dejan Stojanovic said, "Nature is an outcry of unpolished truth."[4]

I can personally testify that when I am in the wilderness, I find all my senses are sharpened—sights, sounds, smells, and senses all become more concentrated for me. In those vast silent places where I have been privileged to walk frequently in my lifetime, I often feel my life is reduced to rudiments of reality. I feel myself going deeper with only one agenda: staying vibrant, staying vigilant, and staying

The Thunder Poet

alive. There, I tend to see more, hear more, and even believe more. In those solitary places, certainties about God and His Word have been revealed to me like no other place on earth.

As I write this paragraph I am in a small cabin deep in the mountains of Colorado. My wife Shirley and I have spent our time this week communicating with God in the mornings and photographing moose, elk, and deer in the afternoons. The cabin is completely off the grid and is powered by solar energy alone. It is a quiet place—quiet enough to hear the voice of the Father without the distractions of a hurried pace. Perhaps that is why Nancy Newhall said, "The wilderness holds answers to questions man has not yet learned to ask."[5]

A Favored Place for Communication

The Hebrew language is a root-structured system of communication. That means that all the words based on any given root are always somehow related in meaning, and thus related to one another.

For example, one word related to a Hebrew word that is often translated *"wilderness"* means *"order or harmony."* Thus the wilderness is a place where you can get things in your life in order, a place where you can find harmony with nature and with God.

Another related word means *"to speak."* The wilderness is a place where a person is able to hear God speak, a place free from distractions, interruptions, and concerns. In fact, in Exodus 3:18,

God instructs Moses to tell Pharaoh that he and the people should travel *"three days into the wilderness"* in order to worship God. All indications of that passage are that the wilderness is favored by God as a place for self-revelation because it is a place where the people can be free from disruptions so they can hear what God has to say to them. We often think of the wilderness as a deathly quiet place, but in reality, it is a place where God can speak clearly to us and where He can reveal Himself completely.

One commentator says, "There are many good reasons for getting away to the wilderness, but the most important reason that Jesus called His disciples away from the people into the loneliness of the wilderness was so that they might 'be with Him.' The Lord called these men to follow Him in a relationship of personal fellowship. He wanted to teach them His ways, and that required closeness. He wanted them to learn from Him and that required closeness. He wanted to train them by personal example, and that required closeness. Most of all, He wanted them just to be with Him because He loved them, and He desired their fellowship! Being with Jesus should be the first priority in each of our lives. If we would be like Him, then we must spend time with Him. If we would serve Him like He desires, then we must spend time with Him. Nothing compares to being with Him." (Mark 1:14).[6] God reveals Himself in the wilderness like in no other place on earth.

The Thunder Poet

The Primal Rift

The Bible tells us that following Christ's baptism, He began His ministry with an extended time in the wilderness. Mark, the gospel writer, describes Christ's experience in Mark 1:12-13. *"Immediately, the Spirit drove Him into the wilderness. He was in the wilderness 40 days, being tempted by Satan. He was <u>with the wild animals</u> and the angels began to serve Him"* [emphasis added]. Mark's mention of the *"wild animals"* adds another dimension to God's wilderness communication repertoire and is more than just coincidental. In fact, these verses evoke some significant theological truths. These Biblical truths offer important life lessons we should grasp in our pursuit of rhyming life with God's indigenous design.

The first of these lessons comes from the prominent role that wild animals play in Scripture from Genesis' beginning to Revelation's ending. Man began in the Garden surrounded by every kind of animal. At the conclusion of Scripture John paints a picture of history ending with Christ seated on the throne surrounded by constant adoration. Revelation 5:13 tells us, *"I heard every <u>creature</u> in heaven, on earth, under the earth, on the sea, and everything in them say: 'Blessing and honor and glory and dominion to the One seated on the throne, and to the Lamb, forever and ever"* [emphasis added].

God's kingdom is for all creatures. All the animals as well as mankind are involved. Jesus' mission of messianic redemption goes far beyond the human realm and includes all creation. Paul addresses this specifically in Colossians 1:18-19, *"For God was pleased to have all His fullness dwell in Him, and through Him to reconcile <u>everything</u> to Himself by making peace through the blood of His cross—whether things on earth or things in heaven"* [emphasis added].

As we saw at the beginning of the previous chapter, a second lesson comes from the fact that we can learn so much from even the lowliest of God's creatures, and those examples can directly influence the way we live our daily lives. Jesus continually used these examples in His teaching. *"Be shrewd as serpents and harmless as doves"* (Matthew 10:16). *"Look at the birds of the sky . . ."* (Matthew 6:26). The Old Testament book of Proverbs does the same. *"Go ask the ant, you slacker! Observe its ways and become wise"* (6:6). In fact, in one chapter of Proverbs alone (chapter 30) Solomon uses examples of *"ravens . . . vultures . . . eagles . . . snakes . . . ants . . . hyraxes . . . locusts . . . lizards . . . and lions."* Even the books of the law refer to wild animals this way. Moses compares God to an eagle who *"watches over His nest . . . and hovers over His young; He spreads His wings, catches them, and bears them up on His wings"* (Deuteronomy 32:11).

The wild animal theme runs throughout the entire book of Job, too. In Job 12:7 ff., Job responds to his friend Zophar and says, *"Ask the animals and they will instruct you; ask the birds of the sky and they will tell you; let the fish of the sea inform you. Which of all of these does not know that the Lord has done this?"* The wild animals have many lessons to teach us.

A third important lesson that comes from the animal kingdom teaches us that during the first 40 days of His ministry, Jesus was *"with"* the wild animals. My wife, my children, my staff, those who know me well, and all those who travel with me to Africa during annual Rock Cry Expeditions know that I love to be *"with"* the wild animals. The reason is that being *"with"* them always makes me think of a coming day when the creation will be restored. It reminds me that one day God will heal the great primal rift that exists between mankind and the wild animals.

In Isaiah 11:6-9, the prophet looks forward to the Messianic Kingdom as a time when *"The wolf will live with the lamb, and the leopard will lie down with the goat. The calf, the young lion, and the fatling will be together, and a child will lead them. The cow and the bear will graze, their young ones will lie down together, and the lion will eat straw like the ox. An infant will play beside the cobra's pit, and a toddler will put his hand into a snake's den. None will harm or destroy another on My entire holy mountain, for the land will be as full of the knowledge of the LORD as the sea is filled with water."* This passage paints a beautiful picture of mankind co-existing in harmony with animals throughout the Kingdom.

I look forward to that day, and the Apostle Paul tells us that the animals yearn for that day as well. *"For the creation eagerly waits with anticipation for God's sons to be revealed. For the creation was subjected to futility—not willingly, but because of Him who subjected it—in the hope that the creation itself will also be set free from the bondage of corruption into the glorious freedom of God's children. For we know that the whole creation has been groaning together with labor pains until now"* (Romans 8:19-22).

What are the wild animals yearning for? Verse 19 tells us that they are yearning *"for God's sons to be revealed."* And why are they so eagerly waiting for that time? It is because the Bible indicates that that time is the time when creation will be restored, and the great primal rift will be healed. In fact, one of the primary features of the Messianic Kingdom will be peace among the wild animals. The healing and wholeness of God will be spread over all creation.

Currently, the creation suffers under the curse of the fall of sinful man (Genesis 3:14-19, Romans 5:12). But the Bible describes an original and perfect creation where the animals and the man and woman lived in harmonious fraternity and where peaceful coexistence was a reality for all the animals as well. But then with man's sin, death entered into the world, and everyday life for the animals became one of a daily struggle for survival.

Abe Gubegna (1934-1980), an Ethiopian novelist and playwright, is credited with the following well-known quote. "Every day in Africa a gazelle wakes up. It knows it must run faster than the fastest lion or it will be killed. Every morning a lion wakes up. It knows that it must outrun the slowest gazelle, or it will starve to death. It doesn't matter whether you are

The Thunder Poet

a lion or a gazelle. When the sun comes up, you better be running."[7] That scene unfolds literally every day on the plains of Africa, and because of that and thousands of other daily scenes just like it, the animal kingdom *"eagerly waits with anticipation for God's sons to be revealed."* Currently the animals live in an environment of constant struggle. They are in endless danger from the presence of "fang and claw."

Sometimes when I am "with" the wild animals, I experience their yearning for reconciliation in a very real and tangible way. I remember one particular incident that occurred one day while I was driving through the deep bush of the Hwange National Park.

The Animals Wait

I glanced at my watch as the sun flashed red-orange through the distant tree line. A waft of cool air rushed through the open window of my truck as I passed through a low-lying area of thick acacia thorn jess and bamboo reeds. Spontaneous goosebumps formed on my over-tanned right arm hanging out the window on the driver's side of my Land Cruiser, an unprompted response often triggered by the combination of a day's worth of sunburn and the sudden extreme change of temperature. It was just past 5:00 PM. The shadows were already growing long, running across the ground and seeping into the landscape like dark moisture drops trickling across the surface of a veldt-colored Popsicle. (Note: "veldt" is another name for the African bush.)

Taylor

My destination was Makwa Pan, one of the most Eden-like settings in the park, a place where I've often spent time with God while He puts the bush to bed and where He occasionally invites a lone determined adventurer to watch Him while He does it. Experiencing sundown in those hidden unpeopled places gives the impression of truly being alone with God—not "alone with God" like the formality of entering into the throne room of an earthly king surrounded by his court, but "alone with God" like the intimacy of being invited to sit with the King on a garden bench in His backyard.

By the time I spotted the buffalo, the attack had already begun. Focusing through the foreground of snow-white acacia thorns, I saw the tawny coat of a lioness, awkwardly balanced on the tiptoes of her hind feet, hanging precariously onto the beast with outstretched limbs uncomfortably overextended around the circumference of his barrel band ribcage. Her fish hook claws were embedded deeply in the buff's hide on either side of his spinal column. The brute's eyes rolled in agony as the lioness stood chewing on his backbone, her teeth sliding through his hide like a kid gnawing the chocolate layer off of an over frozen Eskimo pie. Cream-white streaks of fat-covered severed flesh appeared as the thick black covering was peeled back slash by toothy slash.

By the time I brought my truck to a stop, other lionesses from the pride had caught up to their pre-engaged sister, and they too, began their attack. The buff's body lurched violently as he tossed the nearest lion with his horns. His eyes went crimson in their

The Thunder Poet

sockets as pain stabbed his flanks when the sharp barbs of the lions' claws punched through his firehose thick hide and penetrated the muscles just above his ribs.

Froth and blood spilled from the corners of one of the lionesses' mouth, streaming down her gory jaws as she stubbornly refused to release her grip on the big bull's throat. The buffalo reeled, straining instinctively as he attempted to pull back. But then suddenly he braced himself like a nose-twitched horse fearing any further exertion would only increase the agony of his inevitable execution.

It was then that his eyes locked with mine, and he communicated with an unspoken language of pitiful tortured silence that drilled its way into my heart. His gaze formed a doleful word in my mind, "Why?" My sympathetic gaze was the first and the last glimpse of human compassion the huge buffalo had ever experienced. Now, he was dying, and he knew it. And so did I.

Somehow I felt a tinge of guilt that I had had a part in it all. In fact, according to Romans 8:19-21, this determined savagery is directly related to human sin—my sin and yours. The words of the Apostle Paul came to my mind, *"For the creation eagerly waits with anticipation for God's sons to be revealed"* (Romans 8:19).

The Last Line of the Poem

But why does the creation wait for this revelation? Paul goes on to explain that it waits, *"in the hope that the creation itself will also be set free from the bondage of corruption into the glorious freedom of God's children"* (Romans 8:20b–21). The animals are waiting for the last line of the poem to be written in our lives. They are waiting for their delivery from the curse of mankind's sin. They are waiting for the final rhyming of our lives with God's indigenous design.

And when do our lives "rhyme" with that design? Paul tells us that the rhyme occurs as our lives are *"conformed to the image of His Son"* (Romans 8, vs. 29). John confirms this in his first epistle, as well. In 1 John 3:2, he tells us, *"Dear friends, we are God's children now, and what we will be has not yet been revealed."* [But notice.] *"We know that when He appears, we will be like Him, because we will see Him as He is."* Our conformity to the image of Christ is the rhyme of our lives which God seeks with His indigenous purpose. That is the Thunder Poet's intended plan. That is the last line of each believer's life poem.

The Theme of the Poem

But what I want to know is this: if conformity to the image of Christ is the last line of the poem, what is the theme of the poem? What makes up the "body" of life? What is the story of the believer's life really all about? Paul tells us in 2 Corinthians 3:18, *"We all, with unveiled faces, are reflecting the glory of the Lord, and are being <u>transformed into the same</u>*

The Thunder Poet

<u>*image*</u> *from glory to glory; this is from the Lord Who is the Spirit"* [emphasis added].

The purpose of life and the occupation of life is daily "transformation" into the image of God's Son. This is what we call "spiritual growth" and what theologians call "sanctification." Though one day in glory we will be completely *"conformed"* to the image of Christ, the process of rhyming our lives with God's indigenous design comes through daily transformation, learning life lessons through the ministry of the Holy Spirit and the application of God's Word in our lives. Our poem's theme is our final conformation to His Son's image.

Pastor Brian Bell asks and answers in a sermon, "How long does it take to become a Christian? . . . a moment (justification) and a lifetime (sanctification). It is important to note that the God of miracles is not into instant discipleship. Heaven never hangs out a sign that says, 'Overnight transformations. Inquire within!' God does not do overnight makeovers, but over lifetime transformations."[8] Transformation is a process that lasts a lifetime.

The Indigenous Design

In his book WHEN GOD FIRST THOUGHT OF YOU, Lloyd Ogilvie asks a question that is pertinent to our current consideration. "What were you like in the mind of God when He first thought of you?" That is indeed a thoughtful question, and one for which it is essential to find an answer if we are to understand God's indigenous design. Ogilvie goes on to answer that question with a response that is both concise and profound. Only four words, but as powerful as a spiritual punch in the gut—"You were like Jesus!" That's all the Father ever had in mind for each of us who name the name of Christ.[9] The Poet's intended rhyme was that we would be daily transformed into the image of Christ and that ultimately we would be conformed to that image. "You were like Jesus!"—Your personality, your attributes, your gifts, but like Jesus! That was God's indigenous design for you from the beginning.

Years ago, one of my professors at Southwestern Baptist Theological Seminary quoted a former Southwestern theologian W. T. Conner when he said, "Christ is in fact the only person who has ever lived. All the rest of us are only candidates for personhood. Only as we become like Christ, do we become the persons God created us to be."[10] That is God's indigenous design for you. Rhyming life with God's indigenous design is what your life poem is all about.

"Hey, He's Got a Face Like You"

The year 1981 brought about profound change in the life of our family. At the end of that year, in response to a call from God, our family moved to Zimbabwe, Africa, where we served as missionaries and began living a poem, the lyrics of which continue to be lived out in our lives even today. Yet earlier that year, prior to our departure, there was an event that occurred which influenced my life profoundly and left

The Thunder Poet

me with a life lesson that remains in my heart and mind even now.

Longtime friends and others had been coming by our house, visiting to say, "Goodbye," before our departure. One particular evening Shirley and I had guests visiting in our home. Among our guests that evening were some lifelong friends we had known since our college years. They had a little boy who is just older than our son Rye. During the course of our visit I noticed that their son would look at me and then look at Rye who was just a little guy at the time, and who was sitting quietly in his windup swing. Their little fellow would look at Rye and then look at me—look at Rye then look back at me—back and forth. Finally, he looked at me and pointing to Rye, he said, "Hey, he's got a face like you!"

That brought a smile to my face. It made me so happy and proud as a young father. "My son has a face like me! He's got a face like me. Wow! He looks like me!"

After our guests left for home that evening, I must admit I was still thinking about that little boy's comment, "He's got a face like you!" But at last, after I crawled down off that little stool of vanity, I began to think a deeper thought, and this is it: I don't think there ever comes a time of greater joy in the heart of the Lord God Almighty than when someone looks at those of us who name His name and then they look back at Him. They look at us and then back at Him once again—back and forth. Then finally, somehow, somewhere along the way, they look back to the

Taylor

Father and say, "Hey, they've got a face like you."
That's when we know the poem finally rhymes.

Chapter 3

Snake Stories

> *"Snakes! Why'd it have to be snakes?"*
> Indiana Jones[1]

Death waited cocked and fully loaded just beyond the illusion of security that we called our front door. With the disposition of a psychopath on a sugar high and the heartlessness of a random terrorist, the coiled hair trigger broke the moment our pint-sized pooch took his first step outside.

The strike was a rapid blur—twice the speed of the strike of an American diamondback. It singed the cool morning air like a flash fire fueled by turbocharged lightning. The little white dog never had a chance. It was so sudden that the pup never even saw it coming. Two venom-laced hypos hit him just behind the left ear. The tiny animal was stunned and stiffened quickly as the toxic overdose bulged out of the restricted capacity of his petite little veins. A growing pair of glistening liquid beads the color of saffron-spiked Mountain Dew oozed sickeningly from the lethal wounds.

The pup barely made a sound—more of a light whimper than a crying yelp. He was utterly baffled and confused since until this point he had existed in a world where he had only known friendship and love. Now this ghastly attack completely surprised him. He was stunned by shock as well as by pain. Perhaps his last yearning thoughts were for the warmth of his cushioned pillow or the enjoyment of his squeaking toys that lay at the foot of our little girl's bed only a few feet away on the other side of the door—the safe side of the door where he had known the tender touch of her hand. He, himself, had lain there only a few moments before. Now memories of that beautiful world shattered in his brain like a glass falling on the polished cement floor of a fancy Victoria Falls hotel, and the irreparable shards of that reflection retreated from his mind as rapidly as an unheard echo in the forest.

The venom did its work with surprising speed. The little dog convulsed three times and then became rigid, quivering pitifully. Deserted by hope, his bright eyes glazed, and in despondent loneliness of a regretted wrong step, his brief life came to an end.

The snake that day was a huge African puff adder. African puff adders kill more people than any other snake in Africa, up to 32,000 each year, and they produce many more disabilities because of the destructive potency of their bite. Puff adders have an uncanny habit of lying motionless in a path or on a well-worn route of traffic. They refuse to flee like most

The Thunder Poet

of the snakes of Africa. Instead they strike out violently at whatever happens to tread on or near them. In this sense they are indiscriminate evil— equal opportunity assassins. They are stubby, creepy, sausage-shaped masses of muscle who strangely resemble a slightly stream-lined, yet ornately camouflaged version of Jaba the Hut. When they move they don't move with the usual serpentine motion of most snakes. Rather they move in a straight line like a caterpillar or slug, their bodies undulating across the ground like a slow train on the straight line of track just outside the entrance to Hwange National Park, or like a Chinese Dragon manned by an anesthetized parade crew.

The name puff adder comes from the fact that when they are threatened, these snakes will inflate their bodies and hiss menacingly, a clear warning that the intruder should approach no closer. The warning is not without consequence, either. I once tried to assist a young woman who had been bitten on her ankle, near her village in the Simbala hills just east of our home in Kamativi, Zimbabwe. Her leg was swollen so badly, it was to the point of splitting open from her knee to her hip like a hot dog left on the grill too long. Puff adder bites are not a pretty sight.

Our youngest daughter McKelvey had been unable to settle on a name for the little dog, so we had decided to call him "J. P." "Just Puppy! Let's call him, just 'Puppy,'" she had insisted. So, in a moment of moniker mercy Shirley and I had decided to shorten it to "J. P."

J. P. was a city dog, a solid white Maltese we had purchased while on a shopping trip in Harare. Thus, he never really fit into the surroundings of the Zambezi River Valley. He stuck out like a sore thumb against the brown, green, and khaki colors of the bush. Our intended purpose for the diminutive pup was that he merely serve as a companion for our little girl, but when his brief life came to an unexpected end that day, we celebrated his demise as the death of a hero.

J. P.'s heroic status came from the fact that the big puff adder had been lying in wait for whomever or whatever might step out of the house first that day. Had it been one of our family members instead of the dog, the strike would have found its target in the flesh of one of us instead of in him. Today J. P. is interned in an unmarked hero's grave that is covered with an uneven stack of scattered stones on the side of a hill above the Gwayi River in northern Zimbabwe.

"Tell Us Some Snake Stories"

Snake stories! Often as I travel across the country speaking in various places to mission groups and churches, even civic clubs, I am asked to tell African snake stories. Especially it seems, if young boys are present, they frequently say, "Tell us some snake stories."

Though extensive encounters with eerie serpentine subjects seems to be an expectation of those who discover that a person has lived for years in the deep African bush, many people are surprised and

The Thunder Poet

some are even a little disappointed when they discover that snakes are not found behind every plant or beneath every rock in Africa. In fact, during the cool dry season, we seldom see them at all. But then comes December, and with December, the rains, and with the rains, the snakes.

While I by no means consider myself a herpetological expert, to this day one of my favorite entertainment activities is to sit at my backyard fire pit with a group of *"bakuwa"* (non-Africans) and tell snake stories. People just seem to enjoy hearing accounts of these gliding, slithering, creepy creatures that make up our nightmares and cause us to spook at the sight of crooked shadows in the night.

God's Snake Stories

One of the most fascinating revelations of God's Word is that God likes snake stories, too. In fact, snakes are mentioned more than 80 times in Scripture. A lot of people are surprised when they discover that a snake story is actually the context for the most famous verse of Scripture found in all of God's Word. *"For God loved the world in this way: He gave His One and Only Son, so that everyone who believes in Him will not perish but have eternal life"* (John 3:16). Rhyming life with God's indigenous design and becoming the poetic saga that God has in mind for you and being conformed to the image of Jesus Christ begins with a proper and personal response to the truth of verses 14-16 of John, chapter 3. There is no need to try to proceed further until that issue is settled. Life begins by trusting Jesus and by having and experiencing a personal relationship with Him. God wanted so much for us to remember that great truth, He put it right in the middle of a snake story.

Not only that, but God begins the Bible with a snake story, too. The first verse of Genesis, chapter 3 says, *"Now the serpent was the most cunning of all the wild animals the Lord God had made."* Satan took advantage of that cunning disposition to lie to and deceive Eve and to lead her into rebellion against God. Adam soon followed suit. Mankind fell into sin, and the story of humanity's revolt began.

When God pronounced His judgment, the snake was called out for a special degree of punishment. *"Then the LORD God said to the serpent: Because you have done this, you are cursed more than any livestock and more than any wild animal. You will move on your belly and eat dust all the days of your life"* (Genesis 3:14). Whenever we see a snake crawling across the ground or hear a story of one of those fearsome slithering creatures, it is a reminder of the Fall of man and the horrific consequences of sin. Ever since Satan spoke his lies through the serpent, the snake has been associated with sin and rebellion.

How then could the Lord Jesus Christ have associated Himself with the snake when He gave His famous description of redemption to Nicodemus in John, chapter 3? *"Just as Moses lifted up the snake in the wilderness, so the Son of Man must be lifted up, so that everyone who believes in Him will have eternal life"* (John 3:14-15). It all goes back to an Old

The Thunder Poet

Testament snake story that is recorded in chapter 21 of the book of Numbers, verses 4-9: *"Then they set out from Mount Hor by way of the Red Sea to bypass the land of Edom, but the people became impatient because of the journey. The people spoke against God and Moses: 'Why have you led us up from Egypt to die in the wilderness? There is no bread or water, and we detest this wretched food!' Then the LORD sent poisonous snakes among the people, and they bit them so that many Israelites died. The people then came to Moses and said, 'We have sinned by speaking against the LORD and against you. Intercede with the LORD so that He will take the snakes away from us.' And Moses interceded for the people. Then the LORD said to Moses, 'Make a snake image and mount it on a pole. When anyone who is bitten looks at it, he will recover.' So Moses made a bronze snake and mounted it on a pole. Whenever someone was bitten, and he looked at the bronze snake, he recovered."*

No Whining!

Each year, I take a group of volunteers back to Zimbabwe for two weeks of outreach and church planting among the BaTonga people who live in the valley along the Zambezi River. We travel under the name of Rock Cry Expeditions, and our trip is indeed "expedition-like" in manner and design. Often our trips involve long hikes, proximity to dangerous animals, privations, and other challenges and inconveniences. We hang in hammocks and live simply among the people during our time there, and the trip is mostly without the perks sometimes associated with some contemporary "volunteer mission trips." It is not a trip for the fussy, the demanding, or the persnickety. Anyone associated with the trip knows that the number one rule for Rock Cry Expeditions is "No whining!" When attempting to accomplish a significant undertaking for God, nothing is more harmful and irritating than complaining, griping, nitpicking, and whining within the ranks. Nothing is more distracting and harmful to the cause than that, and for that reason, I dislike whining more than anything else. A whining, cantankerous, complaining, self-centered attitude can more quickly disrupt a positive, effective mission trip than any other attitude.

The snake story that is found in Numbers 21 reveals that God has an extreme dislike for whining, too. In fact, God dislikes that attitude so much, He responded to it in the Israelites' case by sending "poisonous" snakes among the people as punishment.

That word, "poisonous" literally means "fiery" or "burning," and it is the same word that is used to describe the order of angels known as "seraphim." The "seraphim" are literally "flame creatures," and the word comes from a verb that means "to burn."

While it is uncertain as to exactly why these snakes were described as "fiery," there are a number of possible reasons for it. The name may have been given to the snakes because of their color. (On a recent trip to Zimbabwe, I encountered a big puff adder that was the color of gleaming gold or polished brass. When he moved, his skin was shining so brightly in the sunshine that he gave the impression of molten gold flowing across the ground.)

The term "fiery" may also have been given to these snakes because of their ferocity. The same word is rendered "deadly" in the Septuagint. Obviously, many of the bites inflicted on the Israelites were fatal. People were dying because of the bites of these snakes.

Finally, the adjective "fiery" may refer to the burning sensations produced by the bite. Viper bites generally produce a severe burning feeling in the flesh, especially near the area of the venom injection.[2]

Israel Got the Point

It didn't take long for Israel to get the point. Snakes were everywhere, and people began to die. God's judgment brought full confession from the people, and they approached Moses, pleading with him to intercede with God on their behalf. Moses came before God, and God told him what to do: *"Then the LORD said to Moses, 'Make a snake image and mount it on a pole. When anyone who is bitten looks at it, he will recover.' So Moses made a bronze snake and mounted it on a pole. Whenever someone was bitten, and he looked at the bronze snake, he recovered."*

God told the stricken Israelites to look to His provision and they would be healed. Trust is no arbitrary condition. Looking to God's provision is essential for healing, salvation, and deliverance.

"Looking?" Why'd It Have to Be "Looking?"

The theologian A. W. Pink explains it well in his EXPOSITION OF THE GOSEPL OF JOHN, "Man first became a lost sinner by a look, for the first thing recorded of Eve in connection with the fall of our first parents is that *'The woman <u>saw</u> that the tree was good for food,'* (Genesis 3:6 KJV). In like manner, the lost sinner is saved by a look. The Christian life begins by looking: *'<u>Look</u> unto Me, and be ye saved, all the ends of the earth: for I am God, and there is none else'* (Isaiah 45:22 KJV). The Christian life continues by looking: *'Let us run with patience the race which is set before us, looking unto Jesus the Author and Finisher of faith'* (Hebrews 12:2 KJV). And at the end of the Christian life we're still to be looking for Christ: *'For our conversation (citizenship) is in heaven whence also we look for the Savior, the Lord Jesus Christ.'* (KJV) From first to last, the one thing required is looking at God's Son."[3]

"Faith is the keynote of the Gospel written by John. The very purpose for which this Gospel was written was that men might believe that Jesus is the Son of God and that believing they might have life through His name (John 20:31). This purpose is everywhere its predominant feature. From the announcement that John the Baptist was sent *'that all men through him might believe'* (John 1:7), to the confident assurance with which the beloved disciple makes the declaration that he knows his testimony is true (John 21:24), the Gospel of John is one long argument, conceived with the evident intention of

The Thunder Poet

inducing men to believe that Jesus is the Son of God and the Savior of all who trust in Him. The word *"believe"* occurs in this Gospel no fewer than ninety-eight times, and either that or some cognate word is to be found in every chapter."[4]

"Looking" at the snake on the pole also illustrates the complete sufficiency of "looking" to Jesus alone for our salvation. Nothing else has to be added. It is purely a matter of faith in God's provision. The Bible is clear about this: *"For you are saved by grace through faith, and this is not from yourselves; it is God's gift— not from works, so that no one can boast"* (Ephesians 2:8-9). Looking on the brass serpent, God's divine remedy for the snakebite, represents the act of solely trusting in the Lord Jesus Christ's sacrifice on the cross for our needed salvation.

As I stated previously, this saving faith is where a life that rhymes with God's indigenous design must begin. It begins with a personal faith relationship with God through trusting in Christ's sacrificial death on Calvary's cross. That is God's one and only provision for a person who desires a personal relationship with Him.

"But, Why'd It Have to be Snakes?"

Snakes were the problem. Why then did God choose the snake symbol as the answer for the problem? It is because the snake represents sin. We recall that sin entered the human race through the serpent that deceived Eve (Genesis 3:1-6). When Jesus died for us He didn't just take our sins; He became our sin on the cross. The snake on the pole represented Christ on the cross. Jesus Christ BECAME OUR SIN. 2 Cor. 5:21 tells us clearly, *"He made the One who did not know sin to be sin for us, so that we might become the righteousness of God in Him."* Our sin was put to death on the cross. Jesus Christ literally paid for our sin with His own flesh and blood.[5]

Here's a truth that we don't often consider. The Bible tells us *"the wages of sin is death."* Without sin, there is no death. It was *"by one man's sin that death entered into the world."* Since Jesus had no sin of His own, He could not have died. Apart from sin, nothing dies. The only way Jesus could have experienced death was to take on all our sins and take them with Him when He went to the Cross.[6]

That is why the bronze snake in the Old Testament book of Numbers is a shocking but superb metaphor for the cross of Jesus. It meant lifting up the symbol of the very thing that was killing the Hebrew people. John used this vivid image to teach us what the death of Christ really means. God took the hated symbol of Roman oppression (the cross) and turned it into the means of our salvation.[7]

So, that bronze snake in the desert was a shadow of Jesus on the cross in several ways. First, consider that the bronze snake looked like a real snake but was without poison. So, Christ became like us, took on our human nature, but did not have the poison of sin in his own life. Second, consider that the snake was not made of precious metal like silver or gold but of common metal. It was made from bronze.

The Thunder Poet

So, Christ left his golden throne of heaven and came to this earth to share in our ordinary human flesh and blood. He became like us in order to identify with us in every way. Third, consider that the snake brought the Israelites healing through God's promises. Christ has brought us healing through hanging on the pole of that cross. With His perfect suffering and death, He has paid for all sin of all mankind and provided the only antidote that redeems us from sin's poison. With His perfect payment for sin He has canceled our sure death in hell to which sin's poison condemned us. Fourth, just as the snake on the pole was the only remedy for Israelites who were fatally bitten, so Christ on the cross is the only remedy for souls bitten by sin.[8]

Jesus didn't merely empathize with us on the cross. He was literally cursed by God for us. The Bible tells us in Galatians 3:13, *"Christ has redeemed us from the curse of the law by becoming a curse for us, because it is written: Everyone who is hung on a tree is cursed."* God can take something awful and repulsive and transform it into an object of deliverance and redemption. In the ancient world, snakes were compelling symbols of both good and evil, healing and harm. Pictures and images from Egypt often portray the earliest pharaohs as wearing headpieces with a hooded cobra on them. The snake was there for a purpose. He was there to protect the mighty pharaoh by spitting venom on his enemies or biting anyone who would attempt to harm him.

The Greek god of healing was Aesklepius. This god had several sanctuaries across Greece; the most famous was at Epidaurus. In recovered images of him, he carried a wreathed snake on his staff. Whenever a person visited his temple, that person would find that the temple was filled with hundreds of slithering, sliding snakes. The superstitious belief of that day was that if a person could sleep inside the temple among those serpents and be accidentally touched by one of the gliding creatures, he would be healed from whatever ailment that was challenging him. The snake thus became a symbol that was closely identified with healing.

Aesklepius had a Sumerian counterpart, and the Sumerian god of healing was said to have walked around with two intertwined snakes on a staff, a symbol that was later adopted by the American Medical Association, a curious image to be sure, and a mystery for many as to why it was adopted. Someone explained it by saying that the two snakes represent both threat and healing. He went on to say, "Many of you who have been through surgery recently know that if you get mixed up with these people (medical doctors and other medical personnel) who work under the symbol of two snakes entwined on a staff, they often hurt you in order to make you whole. Keep that thought in mind."9

Transformed Repulsion

Thus, my original premise—God can take something awful and repulsive and transform it into an object of deliverance and redemption. That is in effect what He did with the snake on the pole. That's

The Thunder Poet

what He did with our "sin" on the cross. God can do that with the most repulsive things in our lives.

Black Mamba

The black mamba is a fast-moving, extremely nervous, lethally venomous, highly aggressive snake that lives its life as a sadistic reptilian ruffian in the plains, savannas, and remote bush areas of the African wilderness. The snake gets its name not from the color of its body but rather from the inky black lining of the interior of its mouth. It has an oblong head that has been described as resembling the shape of a coffin. Its eyes are pronounced round eyes—eyes dissimilar to the slit, nocturnal, housecat-like eyes of a puff adder or python, eyes that are almost human-like, intelligent eyes. It is the longest of all the venomous snakes in Africa and the second longest venomous snake in the entire world. It can grow up to more than 14 feet in body length and can stand half its body length when it strikes. This means that when the mamba strikes, many of its victims are bitten on the face or upper body. Mambas are fast, too. Some have traveling speeds estimated at up to 12.5 miles per hour. No snake is as elusive, deadly, swift, or potent. As little as two drops of venom can kill a person and a mamba can have 20 drops of venom in its fangs. A single bite has enough potency to kill anywhere from 10-25 adults, and the snake very rarely delivers a dry bite. The snake can strike up to 12 times in rapid fire succession, biting its victim repeatedly without ever letting up. It strikes like lightning, and the mortality rate without treatment is near 100 percent. Depending on the nature and site of the bite, death can result at any time between 15 minutes and 3 hours.[10]

Could such a slithering, spooky, bush-monster contain any redemptive potential? Interestingly, one example of a positive contribution made by the mamba comes from proteins in its venom called "mambalgins" that have been determined through research to be an alternative for opiate drugs such as morphine. Many suffering patients grow tolerant of opiates, requiring higher and higher dosages over time, and the opiates often have harmful side effects like nausea, constipation, and drug dependency. Such side effects are not seen with mambalgins. So, even medically, there are some positive contributions to be found. [11]

But the Bible also reveals in Numbers 21 and John 3, that God can take the most hideous, frightening, and intimidating creature and use it for a good purpose as well. In fact, those passages teach us that we not only see Christ revealed as the Good Shepherd in Scripture, but He is also revealed as the Good Serpent, the Deliverer of those bitten by sin.

Gukarahundi

"Gukurahundi," which is Shona for "the early rain that washes away the chaff," and meant to describe a "purging" of rebellion, lasted for four years in the mid-1980's. (Some say it lasted six or seven years; maybe even longer. Shirley and I were in Africa for much of that time and I heard many of the stories.) Gukurahundi was mostly brought to an end when Robert Mugabe and Joshua Nkomo reached conciliation on December 22, 1987, and signed a unity agreement. Although thousands were killed in Matabeleland and in the south-east of Zimbabwe during that time, there was little international recognition of the extensive human rights abuses (described by some as an attempted genocide). It was twenty years before a report was undertaken by the Catholic Commission for Justice and Peace and the Legal Resources Foundation of Harare. Estimates for the number of dead vary from 20,000 to 80,000.[12]

Some say Gukurahundi was brought about by the government's desire to eradicate trouble-making dissidents from the area—left over war veterans, and unemployed soldiers and political activist who began to prey on the people. Others say it was a deliberate attempt by the government to punish those who were not politically supportive of the current regime. At any rate, many innocent people suffered and died during that time of atrocity—of beatings, of murder, of rape, and of pillaging—a time that was later played down and explained by Mugabe as merely as "a moment of madness."[13]

There came a time when the purge expanded. Mugabe's North Korean-trained Fifth Brigade moved still further north to the edge of Tongaland where the rumored plan was that it would move across the homelands of the BaTonga people in the Zambezi Valley of Zimbabwe in much the same tragic way it had decimated other parts of Matabeleland.

Taylor

The following story was told to me by a trusted friend in Zimbabwe, a man who was a resident living at that time on a farm in the precise part of the world where it all took place. He told this story to me as it had been told to him by one of the last white police officers serving as a Zimbabwe Republic policeman, and who himself had been an eyewitness to the investigative portions of the following events and a first responder and investigator on the scene. I have withheld names here as a precaution for the purpose of protection for those involved.

Mamba to the Rescue

A bush-worn military troop hauler made its way east from the little village of Gwayi like a clumsy lumbering ship traversing the face of a vast sea of sand and dust. Grungy churns of powdered soil the color of a brown paper bag full of dirty dishwater spun from beneath the wheels like rolling swirls of pesticide under the wings of a crop-duster. A dense layer of pounded discomfort poured over the lorry's slanted sides and tailgate, soon covering the battle-hardened occupants huddled inside.

The constant noise of the engine's roar, the continued droning of the drive-train, and the persistent screeching of the gritty brake pads were suddenly gagged as the truck moved across the smooth surface of the Shangani River Bridge. A rhythmic "bump-pump" "bump-pump," "bump-pump," sounded under the thick rubber treads as the heavy vehicle crossed the span, rolling across the

The Thunder Poet

expansion seams in its path. Just a few kilometers beyond the bridge, the sound of splashing water garnered smiles from the combatants as the truck plunged through a perpetually warm stream sourced by the Lubimbi Hot Springs. The smell of sulfur coming from the springs brought crude and coarse remarks from their darkened hearts. *"I smell Tongas!"* one shouted in his Shona dialect with a voice of loathing and contempt.

Shortly, the truck rolled into the clean-swept yard of a local tack shop, and the men bailed out of the back, stretching upraised arms as they walked into the store, arrogantly strutting across the stand with no pretense of respect. In a matter of moments they reduced the shop to shambles. They ate every loaf of bread, confiscated every can of bully beef and tinned vegetables, consumed every ounce of liquid in the place, and then loaded every remaining bag of mealie meal into the truck.

After looting the shelves to emptiness, the men mocked and ridiculed the shop owner, and with taunting derision, walked out front once again. The oldest of the men, wearing a tattered red war beret and the most faded of the camo uniforms, was the obvious leader. He barked orders to the others, commanding them to load up in the truck once again. The driver hopped into the front seat, inserted the key, and readied himself to leave.

Meanwhile the leader scanned the area with his piercing gaze, glancing about for any signs of challenge. Glaring in the direction of a small hut just beyond the shop, he spotted an old woman and her grand-daughter seated on a reed mat in the narrow shade of a thatched roof. They were weaving baskets to sell to tourists who might stop by the store on their way to Binga for fishing—the same kind of baskets as those inside the shop that the soldiers had just ripped to shreds with the sharp ends of their bayonets. One of the cruel men bantered with his fellow soldiers by wearing one of the baskets on his head like a Chinese straw hat as he climbed back into the bed of the truck. The basket-hat was a disdainful trophy of brutality and the conquest of these "Tonga dogs." It had taken the old woman two days to make it, but the loss of its price, if it could have been sold to a traveler, meant continued starvation for the two destitute women.

Then the leader shouted, *"Ewe! Ewe! Huya kuno, imbwa! Huya kuno chikweya!* "Hey you! Hey you! Come here, you dog! Come here, you slow moving old dog!" Focusing on the young woman he shouted, *"Ewe! Ungande kutamba? Huya kuno, bete! Huya kuno, furu!"* Hey you! Would you like to dance with me? Come here, you cockroach! Come here, you maggot!"

With that, the old woman stood up and wrapped her Zambia cloth tightly around her waist as she and her grand-daughter moved slowly toward the soldiers. She cast her eyes toward the ground, refusing to look at the men, more out of terror than out of respect. The leader smirked and winked a menacing eye as he looked over his shoulder to his companions. All the other soldiers by this time had climbed back into the truck.

The Thunder Poet

Squinting toward the woman and her granddaughter and raising his head in disgust, he spoke once again. *"You are the two we have heard about. You are the two that have befriended the opposition! We know you have fed them. Do you know what we do to people who side with the opposition? Ask those people at Lupane." . . . No!"* he laughed, *"That's right, you can't ask them. They are all dead and are rotting where we left them nearby their wells. We left them with their goats and cattle and donkeys. We shot them all until our rifle barrels were glowing red with heat, then we hacked the remainder with our machetes. That's what happens to those who side with the opposition!"*

By this time the women were so overcome with fear, they could no longer control the racing of their hearts. Breathing was a labored chore as the air felt strangely thick and hot. They had heard the stories. They had heard of the horror that came to those who were accused and resisted. Now their time had come. They were so afraid. The older woman had time to utter only a few pleading words, *"No Baba, please!"* They stood helpless before the man, and twenty more pairs of piercing cruel eyes glared at them from the back of the lorry. What awaited them, they feared, was worse than death.

But in that moment, from behind the hut, a streak of movement appeared, a very unlikely glimpse of hope for the women—a completely unexpected turn of events for the soldiers. Like a bright flame surging on a rivulet fuse of dark grey gunpowder, and like fluid mercury rolling elusively across a human palm trying to grasp it, a huge mamba moved with resolute purpose, picking up speed as it raced toward the soldier. At a distance of fifteen feet, the snake's head rose from the ground as its body stiffened like a garden hose lifted by water from an over-pressured pump. Its neck flared as it positioned itself high to strike, and in a moment it was gazing head high and face to face with the soldier who by this time was so awestruck and so overcome with fright that he had failed to even move a muscle. The distance between the soldier and the snake had narrowed from fifteen feet to two feet when at last the soldier instinctively lifted his arm. It was a feeble attempt at protection, an insufficient move that came far too late. Just as his arm started up, the mamba hit him hard, the fangs glancing off his jawbone, sinking deep into the flesh of his right cheek. Though the fangs penetrated instantaneously, the soldier felt the broadening pressure of the sharp injection as the venom squeezed into his face. Before he could retreat, the snake hit him again, this time directly on the side of his nose, then again on his upper neck.

  After the strikes, the gigantic snake raised itself even higher, this time gawking into the soldier's eyes as if scrutinizing his fear, hissing in contempt. The iridescent scales flashed on the flattened neck of the slender monster, and that distinctive blue-black mouth that so characterizes a mamba—that ghastly, cavernous, unnerving mouth, now formed a deep dark backdrop that highlighted the contrasting yellow stream of venom and saliva still dripping from its fangs. The weak-kneed man staggered slightly, then fell back landing on his backside, sitting with his legs spread forward, starring with disbelief in the direction of the retreating serpent making its way unhindered into the bush.

The dismayed soldier's end began with huge drops of sweat breaking out on his brow, the trickling streams of perspiration flowing down his face were hardly felt as his skin began to grow numb. His lips tingled with a Novocain-like sensation and his mouth filled with a strange taste of metal. He tried to focus his eyes on the women standing above him, but double vision plagued his sight, the images seemed neither clear nor real. He drooled shamefully and uncontrollably like a severely handicapped child. Dignity escaped him as his muscles convulsed while his limbs jerked wildly, his body shaking violently as the venom course through his veins and as he lost control of his functions. Paralysis then set in and he could not move his arms or legs or even roll over to attempt to crawl away. There was no escape now. His eyelids drooped and sagged—he could no longer hold them open. From those eyes, his ears, his nose, and every other opening in his body, he felt the warm flow of his own blood puddling to make crimson mud as it mingled with the hot taupe-colored sand beneath him. His attempts at breathing became very tortuous. His lungs tightened like wet rhino hide drying in the sunshine. Then he stiffened drastically and fell backwards, burying the back of his head deeply in the sand as he arched his back in anguish and clenched his teeth until his canines shattered. Then, his body grew still. His death by mamba bite had been like a head start into hell for the soldier—a preview of eternal damnation—a seventeen minute inside track to ageless agony for his crimes against humanity!

As a spellbound witness of the unfolding events, one of the younger soldiers shouted from the back of the truck, *"Huroyi!"* *"Witchcraft!"* Panic ensued, and pandemonium ruled. A terrified and superstitious driver immediately turned the ignition key, put the truck in gear, and drove away without even looking back. Ironically, they left the soldier's body lying there in front of the Lubimbi bush store just like they had left the bodies of the victims of Lupane where they lay after the massacre.

Gukurahundi had come to an end in the Zambezi River Valley. It never returned to Tongaland after that day. But as the lorry raced westward back toward the Gwayi, across the Shangani River, and down the narrow bush paths that led to the main road many miles away, whenever a twisted grey limb or vine from an overhanging tree would brush across the side of the vehicle, or fall into its bed with the occupants, or even cast a shadow from the light of the fading sun, the soldiers screamed. Then silence seized their anxious throats and they dared not look backwards as with terror they mused and pondered on the events of Lubimbi.

What a Snake Story!

Admittedly it is difficult to reconstruct all the events that actually took place that day. It is hard to

The Thunder Poet

distinguish the true occurrences from legendary tales that always develop and accompany episodes like that. All I can say is that it represents the major events of the story as it was told to me. Something happened that day that radically changed the course of Gukurahundi and it illustrates this important truth: God can take something awful and repulsive, something hideous and terrifying, and transform it into an object of deliverance and redemption. *"Just as Moses lifted up the snake in the wilderness, so the Son of Man must be lifted up, so that everyone who believes in Him will have eternal life"* (John 3:14-15). The cross of Christ was a curse to those who refuse to believe, but it is the door of life for those who trust in Him. *"The message of the cross is foolishness to those who are perishing, but it is God's power to us who are being saved"* (1 Corinthians 1:18). A life that rhymes begins with looking in trust to God's provision. *"Just as Moses lifted up the snake in the wilderness, so the Son of Man must be lifted up. . ."* What a snake story! What a glorious hope!

Chapter 4

The Sapient Safari

"Goals transform a random walk into a chase."
Mihaly Csikszentmihalyi [1]

Near the South African town of Hoedspruit there is a safari camp known as *Africa on Foot*. Guides offer "walking safaris" that are billed as "personal and intimate" opportunities to encounter wild game. I agree with that premise since I am convinced that walking is the best and most natural way to see Africa up close and personal. Far too many people travel to Africa and barely even get sand on their shoes. They spend most of their time jumping from the pavement that surrounds their plush hotels into a safari vehicle with cushioned seats and a clever guide that uses a memorized speech to entertain his guests. So much of Africa is missed that way. While viewing game from an elevated perch in the back of a safari vehicle 3 or 4 feet above the ground may provide a degree of safety and security, a person, in order to fully appreciate Africa, needs to touch the earth and feel it separated from the soles of his feet by nothing more than a half-inch of shoe leather. When all is said and done, "walking" is still the finest way to experience the wild and stark terrain known as the deep bush of Africa. I have been privileged to spend many days of my life walking across the veldt, the savannas, and the rugged vast places of Africa. The result of that privilege is that I have come to know Africa in an intimate and personal way. Walking has a way of creating the benefits of intimacy.

The Bible describes the nature of our walk with God in similar terms. In a devotional book entitled SECRETS OF THE SECRET PLACE, Bob Sorge writes, "From the beginning, God has wanted a walking partner. He is looking for not only a clinging bride but also a walking partner. From the very beginning, God had a relationship with Adam and Eve that found them '*walking in the garden in the cool of the day*' (Genesis 3:8). God created man for the enjoyment of a walking relationship."[2]

Many heroes of the faith are described in Scripture as having walked with God. We read of Enoch in Genesis 5:22-24, *"And after the birth of Methuselah, Enoch walked with God 300 years and fathered other sons and daughters. So Enoch's life lasted 365 years. Enoch walked with God; then he was not there because God took him."* And of Noah, Genesis 6:9 tells us, *"These are the family records of Noah. Noah was a righteous man, blameless among his contemporaries; Noah walked with God."* In Genesis 24:40 Eleazar the servant of Abraham describes a conversation in which Abraham told him,

The Thunder Poet

He said to me, 'The Lord before whom I have walked will send His angel with you and make your journey a success. . . ." Of all of these it is said that they walked with God.

The Nature of the Poetic Journey

In Ephesians 5:15-17, the Apostle Paul describes the nature of this walk, *"Pay careful attention, then, to how you walk—not as unwise people but as wise—making the most of the time, because the days are evil. So don't be foolish, but understand what the Lord's will is."* This *"walk"* refers to the poetic saga of a person's experience with the Lord—the distinctive poem of an individual believer's life. According to Paul the believer's walk is intended to be a wise and discerning poetic journey. Thus, I have decided to describe this poetic journey in terms of the wisdom of a sapient safari—sapient describes a journey based on great sagacity, great wisdom or sound judgment, and a traveler, who is discerning, acutely insightful and wise. This describes the nature of the walk that Paul has in mind for the believer.

Wisdom for the Minefield of Life

The Rhodesian Bush War, also known as the Second Chimurenga or the Zimbabwe War of Liberation, was a civil war that took place from July 1964 to December 1979. During that time Zimbabwe inherited around 1.5 million land-mines, mainly anti-personnel mines laid by security forces. These were located in seven minefields, covering 766 kilometers along the Zambian and Mozambican borders. Efforts to clear these mines began in 1980, but residual mines remained for many years. They ran mostly alongside communal lands, where fencing and warning signs were largely destroyed or removed, with devastating results.

One of the most strategic minefields stretched for 220 kilometers from Victoria Falls to the Mlibizi narrows along the southern border of the Zambezi River with 66,000 anti-personnel mines and 22,000 plough-shares initially laid. At the beginning, the Zimbabwe National Army (ZNA) created seven gaps around Victoria Falls, for both human and animal access to the Zambezi and to allow for the maintenance of electricity pylons in the area. In the larger Mlibizi minefield, running along communal and wildlife zones, ten official gaps were cleared. Local people also added a few unofficial gaps.[3]

By 1991 when my family and I moved to Kamativi for our mission work in the area, this section of the minefield had little fence remaining. Often during those days in my travels to remote areas I would see many skull and crossbones signs that remained along the Deka road that runs from Mankuku to Victoria Falls. Also, over the years I heard many tragic stories of people who had been killed or maimed in that area by violent explosions from accidental detonations. In those early years elephants seemed especially susceptible to these explosions. While they were not as often killed as they were merely injured and crippled, when they were injured, their injuries often transformed them into angry and tormented killing machines, striking out at anyone who dared to cross their path. In time they also became adept at avoiding land-mines by sniffing out those lethal weapons from afar. They eventually became experts in avoidance.

Following a Sapient Path

A menacing column of black Matabele ants made its way in single file across a foot worn bush path, leaving tiny tracks in the sand like the crude demarcation of a straight line drawn by a grade school bully warning me not to trespass. I turned east off the main road from Mankuku to Vic Falls, making my way across country toward a village I had been invited to visit by a local headman or "Sibuku" named Mwiimbe. The rumor in the bush was that there was an old cart road which had been used until the seventies that led to the village, but now had become overgrown and unfindable from disuse.

The time was March, 1993. Ndebele Machipisa and I had discussed Mwiimbe's invitation and we determined if we could just reach the village, it would be a fruitful evangelism location. In addition, we would be able to bring much needed food relief to a starving group of people. The only negative factor standing between us and the village was the distance of several miles of dense thick bush and those occasional pesky land mine warning signs.

Taylor

Generally, March brings the end of the rainy season in Zimbabwe, and by that time the bush is normally beautiful, green, and lush, shining at midday like an iridescent speckled wing patch on an emerald spotted wood dove. The year 1993 was different in the Zambezi Valley, and that March came right in the middle of one of the most devastating droughts in the history of the country. The drought had left the bush parched and bare, and the people in the remote villages were starving and hungry. Ndebele and I had a pickup truck bed full of mealie meal that was desperately needed. So I straddled the foot path with the Land Cruiser that day as we made our way off the road into the bush, just beyond the warning signs, assuming there would be a degree of safety if we followed a well-worn path.

The deep bush in the midst of a drought takes on a dry and dusty surreal look—like the surface of Mars covered with a swamp of leafless trees—a reddened sepia surface of wooden skeletal stumps. We made our way through this desolate environment, occasionally commenting on the absence of animals and birds, wondering if we could actually find the village that I had only heard of one day from the Sibuku at the Mankuku store. Things went well for the first forty-five minutes or so as we zig-zagged through the bush skirting downfalls and huge anthills. The path led to a smaller village, but not the one we had started out for. When we asked a small girl in the village for directions to Mwiimbe's village, she simply pointed her finger northeast and said with an ascending voice, "Kule!"—"It is far!" Then she added

The Thunder Poet

words that brought concern – "Kuti ciloto!"—"There is danger there." "Land mines!"

We traveled on with a slight feeling of trepidation. Did the little girl know something of which we needed to be aware? Ndebele sensed my concern and finally spoke, "It has been many years since I have heard of any of those explosions in this area, Mufundisi." "That's good to know, Ndebele," I mumbled back to him while scanning the path ahead for lumps and metal protrusions.

Finally, after traveling for another hour or so, the footpaths faded away. We were too far in to turn around but unsure as to exactly where we were in relationship to our intended destination. I was more than a little concerned.

Just then I looked up to see a young African man walking out of the bush in our direction. (On more than one occasion it seems that God sent a "black angel" to bail me out when I had lost my way. I will be eternally grateful to the wonderful Tonga people for the many times when one of them rescued me from what seemed to be an impossible situation.) After answering his questions about how a white man got a motor car this deep into the bush, I asked him about directions to the village. He pointed to the northeast once again and said, "Pafwifwi." What a welcomed word! It means, "nearby." Then he added, "But Mufundisi, you must be careful. There are land mines in the area and to get through you must find a wide path for your vehicle. When you reach the edge of the escarpment, you will see your destination." Then pointing forward with his spear he added, "You should cross a wide path heading east just ahead." With that I said, "Twalumba kapati."—"Thank you very much." Once again we were on our way.

After another half mile, we encountered a well-worn elephant path, wide and clear, with fresh elephant tracks leading in both directions pressed deep into the powdered sand. I turned right, and traveling eastward now I was amazed at such a fine driving path that the elephant trail provided.

Finally, after following the path along the top of a ridge for another 15 minutes or so, we came to the edge of the escarpment. Looking down we could see Mwiimbe's village surrounded by a clearing where trees and rocks had been removed for crops. We made our way easily from that point to the edge of the homestead. From there I shouted, "Hodi!" (African equivalent to "Knock, knock.") A welcomed voice from inside the nearest hut responded, "Munjile."—"Come in."

Soon we were surrounded by a couple of dozen people. Among them were excited children, some of whom were seeing a white man for the first time. Mwiimbe, himself, was also among them. After polite greetings, he enquired as if surprised, "How is it that you arrived here safely? I thought I might need to come and walk in with you whenever I heard you were in the area" I told him about the little girl and the young man who had provided directions. Then he asked, "But how did you make it through the mines? Your vehicle is large and heavy and wide." I responded, "I followed the trail of the elephants." "Ah!" he said. "The elephants have learned to smell

The Thunder Poet

the scent of the metal in the mines. It's always wise to follow the path of the elephants. Your journey has been a shrewd one."

My journey that day is a picture of life. If you and I are going to arrive safely at the goal of life—if the last line in our life poem is going to rhyme with God's indigenous purpose, the Apostle Paul tells us that we better be certain we are following the right trail. We must follow God's pathway for our life. *"Pay careful attention, then, to how you walk—not as unwise people but as wise . . . So don't be foolish, but understand what the Lord's will is."*

Our Walk

The commentator Hadley Moule commenting on Ephesians 5:15-21 said, "The Christian's walk is no mere promenade, smooth and easy, but a march, resolved and full of purpose, cautious against the enemy, watchful for every opportunity for the King, self-controlled in every habit, and possible only in the power of the eternal Spirit."[4] That definition describes the poetic saga of the believer's life. Following the right path is key to a sapient life safari, and to the experience of wisely rhyming life with God's indigenous design.

In the Greek language, Paul uses the word, *"peripateo,"* for our English word translated *"walk."* That word, *"peripateo,"* actually comes from two smaller words in the Greek—*"peri,"* meaning *"about"* or *"around,"* and *"pateo"* meaning *"to walk"* or *"to tread."* So the word literally means, *"to walk about here and there*" or "*to tread all around.*" It eventually came to mean, "*to make one's way, to make progress, to regulate one's life,*" or "*to conduct oneself.*" Our "*walk*" describes how we conduct ourselves as believers. It describes our life's sapient safari.

Qualities that Characterize Our Walk

Paul qualifies the sapient nature of this "*walk*" in two ways. First, he says we are to "*pay careful attention.*" That concept comes from the word, "*blepo.*" "*Blepo*" means "*to look at, behold, discern mentally, observe, perceive, consider, contemplate, and look to in the sense of taking care, or taking heed.*" It therefore means that we are "*to be on guard*" and "*beware*" as we live out our Christian life. Kenneth Wuest in his excellent work of Greek word study volumes adds that this concept means the believer is "*to see to it that his conduct is accurate with respect to the demands of the Word of God.*"[5] The believer is to give himself to paying continual attention to how he walks before the Lord. He is to walk in strict conformity to a standard.

The KJV of Scripture conveys this idea with the use of the word, "*circumspectly,*" as in "*See to it that you walk circumspectly . . .*" This notion is characterized by exactness, thoroughness, precision, and accuracy. It carries with it the intent of investigating something with great care and alertness. We are to walk warily, exactly, or diligently. Our English word "circumspect" comes from the Latin, "circum" meaning "around" and "specere" meaning

The Thunder Poet

"to look." It literally carries the idea of *"looking around,"* and figuratively the idea of *"being cautious."* It means to walk while being aware of everything going on around you. In the part of the world in Africa where I was privileged to live for all of those years, this wariness is an important discipline to develop. Those who walk around without being aware of what's going on around them are not going to survive long.

The other characteristic that qualifies the sapient nature of our Christian *"walk"* is that we are to *"to walk not as unwise people but as wise."* The Greek word for *"wise"* is *"sophos." "Sophos"* describes the ability to use knowledge for correct behavior. Christians are supposed to walk as *"sophoi"* – *"wise people."* We are to be sapient saints. And the wisdom that Paul stresses here is not theoretical wisdom but practical wisdom that affects behavior. It is not wisdom in theory, but wisdom in practice. It is so characteristic of the practical wisdom that I have observed in the remarkable BaTonga people of the Zambezi River Valley among whom it has been my great privilege to serve.

Sapient Saints

I recall an example of this "practical wisdom" in something that occurred a couple of years ago during one of our Rock Cry Expeditions. I had a wonderful group of volunteers joining me for the trip that year. As always, I was eager to introduce them to the Tonga people that I love so much, and as always, I was a little anxious about how the relationship between the two groups would develop. Because of innate cultural differences between the two groups, I always want everything to go smoothly between them until they get to know each other. I often find myself hoping that nothing happens on either side that might culturally offend or embarrass the other. Until Americans get use to and understand Tonga ways, and until Tongas become acquainted with and understand all of our strange American idiosyncrasies, sometimes things can happen during the course of our visit that are misunderstood or misinterpreted and that have potential to raise questions relationally or spiritually.

We had been in Tongaland for two days and were scheduled to go to a new church start location at a place called Village 21. The reason the village was called by a number instead of a traditional Tonga name is because it is located near the mining town of Kamativi, and thus had been influenced by more western ideas and culture. Admittedly, I was a little suspicious about the prospects of success there because it has been my experience that our best and strongest Tonga churches have been planted in areas that I would call "pure Tonga" areas—areas where there is little or no western influence. But our trusted Tonga leaders had said this was a good location and my experience has also taught me to go with their recommendation whenever possible.

We had a tremendous worship service leading up to a very successful time of evangelism. Our Tonga leaders had obviously done their work in advance and the people were prepared to worship and to welcome our guests. There were a number of new believers

The Thunder Poet

already present who had been lead to the Lord by our African evangelism team and the discipleship process had been started in their lives. They were growing in the Lord and were stepping up to lead us in worship upon our arrival. In those early days of a church's development I'm always a little concerned about outside influences from syncretistic and cultic groups. Heretical and deviating groups sometimes come out from towns close to the more nearby villages and bring with them confusion and heresy, teaching the people doctrine and ways that are not consistent with Scripture.

All went well that evening as we worshipped. The African people naturally worship with a full and open hearts, and they worship with song and celebration until everyone has participated. They know nothing of hymn stanzas that are completed or finished by numerical succession, and their services are not governed by time conscious clock-watchers. They sing and dance uninhibited before the Lord until every person present has had an opportunity to be a part. That night the worship service was in full swing and the celebration was at a full tilt mode as the people danced and leapt before the Lord. A thick cloud of powdered sand rose from the ground and covered the worshipers, clouding the air in our area of worship.

It was then that something caught my attention that caused me to wonder and brought a question to my shepherd's heart about what was going on. Out in front of the pounding feet of the rejoicing young people a little elderly woman preceded them with a shallow dish full of water in her hand. She was scooping handfuls of the water and then she would sprinkle or fling it on the ground just in front of the stomping feet of the young people. It reminded me of what a priest had done one day at my one and only attendance of a Roman Catholic Mass, as he took an aspergillum and hurled water enthusiastically over the crowd. Something just didn't feel right. "What kind of new teaching is this? I'm not sure I'm comfortable with this 'water-sprinkling' ritual."

About that time, one of the American guests leaned into me and asked, "What does that mean?" Frankly, I was not sure. I had similar questions in my own mind. "Is this some syncretic practice that has been imported from one of the local 'town' cults?" "Perhaps this is an attempted reproduction of a Roman Catholic Mass observed by someone who has visited the city?" I knew the American guest needed an answer, and I needed to sooth my puzzled mind, too.

When I could stand it no longer, I leaned over toward my most trusted African leader and asked him, "What's going on here? What is that Bama doing with the water?" You could have knocked me over with a feather when he whispered his answer. "She's dampening the dust on the ground to keep it from choking our guests." *"Duh! Why didn't I think of that?"* There I was trying to figure out some profound spiritual or ritualistic meaning to her actions, and she was just demonstrating practical wisdom.

The Thunder Poet

Wisdom! Sometimes our greatest need is simple wisdom if our life journey is to be a sapient safari. Often practical wisdom is what is needed most.

Our Most Valuable Commodity—Time

In the Ephesians 5 passage Paul stresses that we are to *make the most* of our time. The sapient safari of the believer's life is characterized by a wise investment of time. Time is the most valuable commodity that we have. It is certainly more valuable than money. Somebody said, "Money comes and goes, but time just goes." There are people in this world who would give every penny they possess if they could just buy a little more time. Once spent, however, time is an irrevocable expenditure. It is an irreparable shard of eternity. Our stay on earth is brief. We are here for only an instant, then we are gone. That's why the Apostle James writes, *"For you are a bit of smoke that appears for a little while, then vanishes"* (James 4:14). And the Psalmist prayed, *"Teach us to number our days carefully so that we may develop wisdom in our hearts."* (Psalm 90:12)

Time is Short

While I am writing these lines today Shirley is cleaning out a closet drawer here in our home. She just came across some Christmas cards from last Christmas. Among them are some I've decided to re-read while I sit here at my desk. I have begun to concentrate for a few moments on their message. There are two cards here that have caused me to pause and ponder. The first card is from my mom who passed away at age 92 this past October (2017) and her message is a part of her sacred legacy for my life. I shall forever be grateful to God for His grace gift of godly parents in my life.

Another card that has caught my attention is from a young lady who attended our church here in Pratt, Kansas for a couple of years prior to moving to south Texas to continue pursuing her career. The message of her card is simple yet meaningful and a reminder of many good times of fellowship we experienced with her through our church in the past. Her message reads:

Merry Christmas and many blessings to your family in the new year!
I sure missed your homemade ice cream at Christmastime this year.
I'll be thinking of that for decades.
Thanks for your love and care during my time in Pratt.
The Lord has blessed me so much already here in my new home in Texas.

I am struck deeply by her message and I have gone back to read it once again. The part of it that jumps out at me now are these the words: *"I'll be thinking of that for decades."* The reason those words have gripped my heart so is that that young lady, only in her 20s, drowned while on a camping trip this past

The Thunder Poet

summer. She lived with anticipation of savoring memories we shared for decades to come, but in a moment life for her was over. We must journey with the intent of a sapient safari, wisely *making the most of our time*. We never know how quickly our time may pass.

Yes, Time is Short

While writing this chapter, I went out and bought an hourglass and set it on my desk. The reason I did so was so it could serve as a reminder to me regarding a proper perspective toward time. The circular movement of the hands of a modern clock tends to give us the impression that time just goes on and on. When one 24 hour period is completed, the hands just fluidly keep right on moving into the next. It almost makes us think time is perpetual. Like the ad about the Energizer Bunny, we think time just keeps "going, and going, and going." But the fact is, like the sand in an hour glass, time is running out. One day, for each one of us, time will be no more. We tend to avoid that thought. We deny it, or ignore it, or joke about it, all in an effort to escape its reality, but nonetheless time races on. Last Saturday was my 67th birthday. I wrote this in my journal at the end of the day: March 10, 2018 —

Time is passing quickly now—like the clicking of a meter in a taxi whose passenger is stuck in traffic with less than $30 left in his pocket. I sense an urgency that insists I not spend my time on things that are not meaningful.

Taylor

"I'm a 100 and a Half"

A humorous commentary on aging has circulated on the Internet for a number of years and is said to have been created by comedian George Carlin. While the sardonic humor sounds like that which is characteristic of Carlin, there is no evidence that he ever performed it. However, regardless of its origin, the truth is still there, and it challenges us to think seriously about our limited time and how rapidly it is passing:

"Do you realize that the only time in our lives when we like to get old is when we're kids? If you're less than 10 years old, you're so excited about aging that you think in fractions. 'How old are you?' 'I'm four and a half!' You're never thirty-six and a half. You're four and a half, going on five! That's the key. You get into your teens, now they can't hold you back. You jump to the next number, or even a few ahead. 'How old are you?' 'I'm gonna be 16!' You could currently be only 13, but hey, you're gonna be 16! And then the greatest day of your life . . . you become 21. Even the words sound like a ceremony . . . YOU BECOME 21. YESSSS!!!

But then you turn 30. Oooohh, what happened there? It makes you sound like bad milk! He TURNED; we had to throw him out. There's no fun now, you're just a sour-dumpling. What's wrong? What's changed? You BECOME 21, you TURN 30, then you're PUSHING 40. Whoa! Put on the brakes, it's all slipping away. Before you know it, you REACH 50 and your dreams are gone. But wait!!!

The Thunder Poet

You MAKE it to 60. You didn't think you would! So you BECOME 21, TURN 30, PUSH 40, REACH 50 and MAKE it to 60. You've built up so much speed that you HIT 70! Sounds like you've run into a wall. And it doesn't end there. Now you're into your 80's or 90s. But then a strange thing happens. If you make it over 100, you become a little kid again. 'I'm 100 and a half!'[6]

The Bible teaches that we should make each day count, and that we should learn the value of each day by *"redeeming the time."* Our time on earth is short and the duration of our life is but a moment compared to eternity. The time of our life is such a valuable treasure, we cannot afford to waste even one day. We should therefore *"make the most out of"* every day that the Lord chooses to give us to live. God has set boundaries for our lives and everything we do must be done within those boundaries. We want to talk about spending time, but the Bible talks about buying it up and investing it. Eternity will magnify what we have done with the gift of time in our lives.

An Over-Burdened Life

Two things are implied when it comes to *"making the most of our time."* First, we must be certain we establish the right priorities. For many people, life is just too full of an abundance of events and activities. Some people, it seems, try to do everything and take advantage of every opportunity, and therefore, they end up with too much on their plates. This lack of choosing priorities costs them in at least two ways.

For example, there are those individuals whose life-poems are marred under the weight of an overburdened life. They are far overcommitted with their schedules, and in an attempt to do everything, they end up doing nothing very well. We must choose our priorities or risk endangering ourselves with a life that never rhymes.

Too Much Weight Sinks a Ferry Boat

I once saw a strange sight while crossing the Kafue River in Zambia. There is no bridge there—or at least there was none there at the time—so since the Kafue is deep and wide, all traffic must cross the river by ferry. One day as I sat awaiting my turn to cross, I watched with amazement as two dump trucks, heavily loaded with marigold flowers from nearby plantations on the Zambezi, came to the river and pulled out onto the deck of the crude wooden ferry boat. All seemed to be going well at first, but then as the ferry neared the middle of the river the crude vessel slowly began to sink under the weight of its load. By the time it got to the very center of the flowing waterway, nothing was left visible but the tops of the heaps of flowers in the back of the vehicles and the yellow and orange residue drifting slowly downstream. The ferry was completely immersed, sinking under the tremendous weight of the load.

I failed to reach my destination that day; however, I learned a vital lesson. Some people try to do the same things with their lives. Attempting to carry too heavy a load and never saying no while trying to be involved in too many activities of life, they sink beneath the currents of mediocrity known to those who never establish priorities. Their life-poem is marred by an overburdened life.

Choices

Another consequence that comes from and over-full life is that there are those people whose life poems are ruined because they make wrong choices, or refuse to make choices at all. Years ago, I came across some very practical advice given in a commentary by Wayne Barber on how we can "redeem the time." He tells us that the term "*redeem*" means to "*purchase time.*" But to purchase time you "have to have collateral. Not only do you have to have collateral, but you have to have the right kind of collateral if you are going to purchase anything. So what is the collateral used to purchase time? It is my choices."[7] According to Barber, choices make up the needed collateral for our purchase of time.

We only get one time around in life so we have to be sure we make the right choices. The colloquial phrase is that we have to make certain that we "get the most bang for our buck." That phrase is an idiom meaning the worth of one's money or exertion. We must learn to get the most significant payoff in our lives from the time and effort we have invested in it.

Impala or Buffalo?

We can learn a lot from watching an African lion capturing and killing its dinner. Given the choice, a lion prefers buffalo over impala. That is not necessarily because buffalo meat is more delicious than impala meat. (Though having eaten lots both of them, I would have to admit that buffalo meat definitely has the edge on flavor.) Yet for the lion, flavor alone is not the basis of his decision. It comes down to the fact that the chase requires the same effort regardless whether it is a buffalo or an impala. The amount of meat, however, is much greater if the prey is a buffalo. So, when it comes down to choices, lions choose the "most bang for their buck" and take advantage of the best reward for their effort. Choices involving time are often not between the good and the bad, but rather between the good and the best. Rhyming life with God's indigenous design requires a sapient safari.

Unfortunately there are people who focus on things of lesser value—things that don't matter in light of eternity. That's possible for any of us to do, especially if we hold the things of this world too dearly. We have to make a deliberate choice to value things that genuinely matter with the priority they deserve.

Poor Choices = Wrong Priorities

Our last term as career missionaries in Africa was spent on the north side of the Zambezi River. We

The Thunder Poet

had been denied work permits in Zimbabwe, so we lived out our final term in Zambia in a little fishing village called Siavonga. We were privileged to live right on the banks of Lake Kariba which is made up from the backwater of the Zambezi River. Siavonga is an extremely hot place and not many people choose to live there for that reason. However, one of the benefits of living there is an opportunity to be contiguous to water and to fish there in the lake, if a person chooses to do so.

With that expectation and the anticipation of that privilege in mind, prior to leaving the USA for our final term I had invested in some excellent fishing equipment—nice quality rods and reels as well as fly fishing tackle. The equipment was more expensive than I imagined it would be, but I was committed to take good care of it and planned to use it for many years. I had looked forward to those times of fishing on the lake, but as it turned out, there was not nearly as much time for fishing trips as I had originally imagined. There always seemed to be another village somewhere further down the lake waiting and needing someone to come and share the gospel. There just didn't seem to be much time for the less important opportunities of fishing for fish when there were so many opportunities for fishing for men.

However, one day I received a call from our mission headquarters in Lusaka, telling us that there were some volunteers coming out from the USA who desperately wanted to do some mission work on the Zambezi River. Shirley and I had been chosen to host the volunteers. In addition to the mission opportunities that would be afforded to them by working with us, they also desired to see the beautiful part of the world where we lived, and it turned out that one of the young men in the group had a lifelong ambition of catching some tiger fish in the Zambezi. While I hadn't had a lot of time for that endeavor, it seemed like a great chance for me to break out all that fantastic, yet seldom used, fishing equipment that I had brought over from the states.

It was a terrific day and our neighbors, the Peiterses, who were river safari guides, went along with us and brought their houseboat, too. That way we could all fish on the huge deck and stand in a shoulder to shoulder, next to each other, good for conversation and fellowship, type of formation. I even loaned the young volunteer fisherman my best rod and reel. As I handed it to him I said, *"Take good care of it."* He used it well, too. He caught Tigers and Kariba Bream that afternoon, as well as a few other lake fish. He learned what we all had learned about Zambezi fishing—while reeling in a fish, a person has to race the crocodiles that are determined to steal as many as they can from successful fishermen.

All the fishing and splashing had created a lot of excitement among the huge reptiles and after a while they would go for anything flopping on top of the water. Crocodiles were all around, and by late afternoon our sport of fishing had morphed into another sport—an exercise in racing crocodiles, the sport being the challenge of who could best get the fish in the boat before a crocodile snapped it up. Previously caught, injured fish and fish bitten half in

The Thunder Poet

two, added lots of blood to the water and the crocodiles seemed to be enjoying the afternoon as much as we were.

All was going well. A few hippos, lots of fish, lots of crocodiles, lots of good times and good memories had combined to make a great day and a relaxing experience for all of us.

Then something happened that changed all of that. The young American volunteer drew his arm back dramatically, and with a long smooth cast he shouted, "*Watch the distance of this cast.*" As the rod came over his shoulder and as he released the line, from my vantage point everything seemed to change to slow motion. In fact, I could hardly believe my eyes. In an effort to make an outstanding distance cast, he had let go of both the reel and rod, and my super-duper American made rod and reel was flying from his hand out over the water. It went sailing right into the lake with a splash. With a stare of unbelief, I could see my prized fishing rig slowly sinking like Jack Dawson from the wreckage of the *Titanic*, the loose filament line still floating on top of the water.

I'm not sure that I can recall exactly what I was thinking at the moment, but without thinking I put my hands up on the rail of the boat and with one whirling dervish leap I jumped right in. I do recall Shirley's shout as I was soaring through the air, "*The crocodiles, Steve!*" Too late! Poor choice! Wrong priority! I was already committed. I sunk faster and deeper than I had imagined into the water's depths, but fortunately my hand hit the floating filament which I grasped on my way in.

To make a long story short in an understated fashion, I made haste getting back into the boat and I learned yet another one of my valuable lessons that day. My lesson was this: while I have never had enough faith to actually walk on water I've learned that given enough motivation and enough crocodiles in the water, a person can produce a rather reasonable facsimile of it. Anyway, I got back in as quickly as I could.

Certainly a more valuable lesson is this: it is entirely possible for a person to make a wrong choice when it comes to priorities. We can sacrifice the value of an eternal priority by jumping after temporal things that in comparison are worthless. My foolish spur of the moment decision could have cost me God's intended ending for my life-poem. *"Making the most of our time"* means establishing the right priorities.

A Sacred Opportunity

A sapient safari involves our response to a sacred opportunity. In his sermon, "Watch How You Walk," Ray Pritchard, says that the word translated here as *"make the most of," "redeem,"* or *"buy up,"* is a word from the marketplace. He writes, "It describes going down to the supermarket and looking for bargains because you know they will not last long; they are passing and changing. Therefore make the most of them and buy them up" while you can.[8] Regardless, the sapient safari is characterized by recognizing the value of time, the fact that it is limited, and making the best possible use of it through wise priority-based choices. It means seizing worthy opportunities that come our way.

There are actually two Greek words in Scripture that are translated "time." One word is the word "*chronos.*" *Chronos* refers primarily to the duration of time as in the succession of minutes. It designates a period or space of time, and we even have words in our English language that are built from that Greek root—chronology, chronograph, chronometer, to name a few. The other word for time is "*kairos.*" *Kairos* refers not to the duration of time but rather to a period of opportunity, a space of time that is filled with all kinds of opportunities—a significant moment. *Kairos* is the word Paul uses in the passage in Ephesians 5. "*Time*" for the Apostle Paul is "*a period of opportunity.*" It is a "*ripe moment.*" It refers to "*the best time to do something.*"

The theologian John Broadus said, "Opportunity is like a fleet horse that pauses for a moment at one's side. If you fail to mount him in that moment, you can hear the clatter of his hoofs down the corridors of time. That opportunity is gone forever."[9] Historians write of Hannibal that when he could have taken Rome he would not, and when he would he could not.

Every person has one life to live in this world, and then it is over. How we live and what we accomplish for Christ is determined by deliberate choices to follow God's will for our lives. I began this book with a statement of faith and fact; each life has a mission and a purpose. Each one of us is a life that is a unique and an original poem written by the hand of the Thunder Poet Himself. The only way to live out that life is to live in response to God's direction, purpose, and call. Once you determine that purpose by understanding God's will for your life, it is your responsibility to embrace and grasp your purpose and live it out in the fullness of the presence of God. To ignore or waste that gift is an insult to the Giver.

Understanding

Embracing and grasping your purpose is why understanding God's will and purpose for your life is so important and why Paul commands it in his passage. Your understanding represents the point at which life *"comes together"* for the believer. In fact, the word he uses for *"understanding"* means *"to send together or bring together."* The idea is to put together pieces of a puzzle. In Ancient Greek, Homer used the word to describe two rivers flowing together. The idea is that of an individual getting the big picture of what his life is supposed to be about. Once you have that picture, you must recognize that you only have the time allotted to this, your one and only life, and that you should grasp it and be about it in this world.

The intrepid missionary Adoniram Judson once said, "A life once spent is irrevocable. It will remain to be contemplated throughout eternity. The same may be said of each day. When it is past, it is gone forever. All the marks which we put on it, it will exhibit forever. Each day will not only be a witness of our conduct, it will affect our everlasting destiny. How shall we then wish to see each day marked with usefulness? It is too late to mend the days that are past. The future is in our power. Let us, then, each morning, resolve to send the day into eternity in such garb as we shall wish it to wear forever."[10] Are you *understanding* and grasping that kind of purpose and potential for your life today?

One Chance to Grasp a Life

The destination for the day was Nanjili. The people there had been increasingly responsive to the gospel, hungry to hear God Word, and deliberate about growing in it. On the previous Sunday I had spent 7 hours with them. I had begun teaching at 9:00 AM and they were still asking questions at 4:00 PM. To this day, of all the places I've ever taught God's Word, that village stands out as one of the most anxious to learn more about the things of God. By the end of that afternoon I had promised that I would bring Tonga Bibles back as soon as possible, and now it was Thursday morning and that project was my plan for the day.

I had approached Shirley the night before with this proposition; *"Tomorrow I'm heading up to Nanjili. It's only a couple of hours up river and I only have some Bibles to deliver. We can leave Siavonga by 9:00 o'clock and be back by dark. Would you and McKelvey like to go along with me on the trip up the Lake? We can eat lunch aboard the boat near Nanjili and have a good day traveling on the river."*

The International Mission Board had provided a well-used, almost antique, 21-foot cabin cruiser that made the trip easy. I kept the boat moored at the Pieterse Harbor and it would just be a matter of backing out and heading up river.

We started the day leisurely and loaded up about 9:00 AM. By 9:30 we were out of the harbor, past the first barrier of hippos, and on our way. We raced egrets and cranes that took flight ahead of us. Distinctly silhouetted against the ragged green canopy of teak and mopane trees that lined the banks of the river, they looked like determined escorts as we made our way up the lake. Occasionally a huge croc would slide into the water, feeding smoothly into the eddied current with the fluid motion of a giant brass shell loading into the guns of a battleship. No worry to us. We felt safe on our island of sprinting fiberglass, sheltered in the imaginary security of our modern river transport. With wind blowing in our hair—that is, in Shirley's and McKelvey's hair, and across the top of the leather tanned skin that covered my head—we laughed and talked and had a great time for the duration of the trip. We slowed only for the occasional fisherman in his dugout canoe who happened to cross our path or to skirt a random bleached skeletal tree trunk and the bare branches of dead trees that were drowned when the river was damned all those years ago. Those trees make excellent perches for fish eagles, cormorants, and other water birds, but they also collect the webs of huge spiders that can be rather unpleasant to run through in the semi-dark.

We arrived at Nanjili by 12:00 noon and shared our lunch of peanut butter and jelly sandwiches, Mazowe orange drink, and packages of some un-

The Thunder Poet

recalled weird flavor of Willard's Potato Chips with the young men who were sent by the headman, now church leader, to collect the boxes of Bibles that I had brought on board. We spent the afternoon in conversation with those young men who in typical Nanjili style were full of questions regarding their new-found faith. There is hardly a more pleasant recollection from our years in Africa, than the sight of watching those young men with boxes on their heads, making their way back up the rocky hill to their village, singing new-learned songs of praise as they travelled along, rejoicing over their treasured possession of the Word of God.

It was 4:00 PM by the time we departed, and we had scheduled just enough time to make our way back to Pieterse Harbor by dark. I carefully dodged tree stumps and rock outcrops that are numerous in the Nanjili inlet and kept the engine of the big cruiser at idle as we made our way toward the mouth of the inlet. I glanced at my watch and that circuitous maneuvering had taken more time than I had expected. It was already almost 5:00 by the time we came to the body of Lake Kariba. I decided to pick up a little speed and with my right hand I reached down and pushed the throttle forward. The cruiser responded by thrusting its nose into the air. Leveling out, I watched carefully for obstacles that might be sticking above the water, and I held tightly to the steering wheel knob located on the wheel. (This was one of those classic steering wheel knobs like you would see on a 55' Chevrolet—it had a joker's face on it and a red hat complete with three bells hanging off the pointed peaks—a friend who restores vintage vehicles had sent it to me from the states to make my long hours of travel up and down the Zambezi more easy to steer.)

As we sped along, suddenly and unexpectedly, the knob jerked from my hand and the cruiser lunged sharply to the left. We had collided with something submerged, and the impact was rapid and severe. Instinctively, I reached down and pulled back on the throttle. The bow of the boat plunged downward with the cushioned deceleration of the ill-timed landing by an awkward mallard. The engine made that "suddenly shut down" motorboat noise like an overweight tuba player mimicking the role of a toddler rudely blowing air through his milk with a straw at dinner time.

A quick examination revealed that the steering mechanism was completely broken. The wheel and the knob just spun freely in every direction in my hand without any connection to the rudder at all. Though I attempted to make initial repairs, failure soon revealed that the solution was far beyond my mechanical ability. It was after 5:00 PM now and we were still two hours from home even if we were able to travel at full speed. With the steering mechanism broken, it was going to take a long, long time.

Fortunately, I had a little 2 ½ horsepower Johnson motor hooked on the back of the boat, just in case I had such emergencies. Having switched off the primary engine, I now pulled on the rope to start the little motor. To our delight it cranked on the second pull and we were on our way at a snail's pace as the little engine strained to push the heavy weight of the

The Thunder Poet

cruiser. What had been planned as a pleasant and leisurely enjoyable afternoon was rapidly degenerating now into the prospects of an all-night affair. As long as I could stay awake, keep refueling the little engine, and keep heading in the right direction we would at least make progress toward our destination. Finally, we made it out to the main channel and I turned east to head back down the river toward Siavonga and our home there. A gentle east wind was blowing from that direction toward us, but as long as it stayed "gentle" we should be able to make progress.

By 9:00 PM the wind was no longer gentle. Lightning was flashing on the horizon in the east and waves began to beat rhythmically against the bow of the boat. Progress was going to be much slower. Lake Kariba's weather is generally benign during the dry months with clear skies and prevailing easterlies that may be replaced by localized on-shore breezes from late morning onwards. However, when an evening storm rolls down the Lake and winds up to Force 8 or more, steep seas and near-zero visibility during rainstorms may occur. Lake Kariba is 140 miles long and 25 miles wide at its widest point. That's bigger than some bodies of water that are called seas. Storms can be forbidding and severe. Alert skippers had warned me to watch for the development of such storms well in advance, and to run for shelter. "If that is not possible," they had said, "stay well offshore and try to hide behind an island on the off side from the wind. That's the only hope of riding it out."

Taylor

By midnight-night the situation had deteriorated considerably. The waves were so big now that the boat was bucking like a two-year-old colt under its first saddling and was making no progress against the wind at all. Shining a search light on the north shore, I could tell at times that we were sliding backward, and I feared we might be dashed against the rock bank of the north shore of Kariba. (A little-known fact, unless you have reason to know: On average crocodiles are found approximately every 100 meters on the banks of Lake Kariba. I had reason to know!)

I began to realize that unless the weather broke soon, we were not going to make it. It was time for a decision. Again, shining my light to the south I could see that there was an island just behind us to the south and the west, not more than a few hundred yards away. I shouted to Shirley, *"I'm going to try for it."* With the waves so large now that I feared capsizing, I decided to make the turn as quickly as possible in order to avoid being broadside against the wind for too long. However, when I pushed the motor handle behind me it seemed to take forever for the bow to come around. Finally, we were turned diagonally away from the wind and were once again making good time towards the back of the island. I deliberately went across the front of the island first, so I could turn in behind it and have calmer waters with which to navigate. Again I shouted to Shirley, *"When we get behind the island, you'll need to grab a limb on one of the dead trees standing in the water. Tie off as quickly as possible. With the wind blowing like*

The Thunder Poet

this we may not get a second chance. I'll hold the motor in place and try to give you as much time as possible." Shirley and McKelvey were huddled under the canopy near the steering column trying to stay out of the storm, but when her eyes caught mine, she could tell I was very serious and she began to prepare to make her way to the front of the boat where she would have to stand on the deck, grab the limb, throw the rope around the tree and tie off as quickly as possible. No small task, even for my wife who over the years I had come to know as a super hero disguised as a 5-foot, 2-inch, blonde-haired, blue-eyed cutie. Though she doesn't really look the part, during those years in the bush, Shirley always seemed to find a way to get things done.

Now I was in a position to make a run on the "reduced-wind" side of the island and I spotted a sturdy looking bleached dead tree that was going to be my target. With McKelvey still huddled under the canopy and Shirley standing on the deck with a tie off rope draped around her neck, I breathed a final prayer and made my run toward the tree. At first I thought I might have to slow down to keep from running over it, but as the wind picked up and the waves pushed harder against us I began to question whether we would make it at all. Again I shouted, *"You may only have one shot at this. Make it count!"*

"Slowly! Slowly! Closer! Closer! Now stretch!" We were there. She reached for a limb, but the momentum of the dropping boat bow snapped it quickly in her hand. Again I shouted, *"You'll have to throw the rope around the tree."* With a lunge and a

quick loop that would make a mediocre calf-roper blush, she did it like a pro. At last we were secured against the storm. With the rope now in place around the tree, I switched off the engine and made my way to the front of the boat where I let out some length from the rope to add some flexibility and tied off the knot so we could wait out the night. Our "one shot," had paid off. We had made the most of our "ripe moment." We had "redeemed the time" and we were able to make it through the night on Lake Kariba.

The reason I've told you this story is to remind you that you get one shot at this life—one shot at an opportunity to make a difference for eternity—one shot to discover and live out God's purpose and the reason for which you were born. Have you determined to make your safari a sapient one? Is the poem of your life rhyming with God's indigenous design?

Chapter 5

Plagiarized Poems and Passionless Lives

"Today you are you! That is truer than true! There is no one alive who is you-er than you!"

Dr. Seuss[1]

God never plagiarizes His poetry. When He composes, He always pens an original verse. Each person's life is an original expression of His creative artistry, and every element of His artistic composition is authentic and unique. Like human fingerprints, snowflakes, zebra stripes, and the irises of human eyes, His poems rhyme, but they never reduplicate. Each is always a one of a kind, singular, solitary work of art.

Therefore, one of the greatest tragedies of life comes when instead of living out our intrinsic singularity we begin trying to mimic the life of another. Whenever that occurs, the poem is marred and the purpose for our individual uniqueness is impaired. Biographical plagiarism is a deviating insult to the plan of God. Because of that the Thunder Poet builds individuality into each of His creatures as an example of its importance in the lives of His people.

Even the Elephants

That is the case even when it comes to the mighty African elephants. No two are identical or exactly the same. Did you know that each of them even has a unique voice? We can learn much from the acoustical communication of the vast herds. I have often heard them late in the evening while waiting at waterholes or at night nearby my camp in the Zambezi Valley. One night at Saba while lying in my tent, the light of the moon disappeared in the middle of the night even though the moon was still hanging high in the sky. It turned out that an elephant was standing so nearby right over my tent I could hear the low rumbling of his voice above my head.

Elephant voices are amazing. Elephants use their voices to communicate in a number of ways. They communicate with one another to warn each other of potential dangers, organize the group, attract elephants of the opposite sex, secure defense, and reinforce family bonds. They also vocally communicate their needs and desires to other members of the herd.

The basic language structure of the elephant is thought to comprise 70 or so vocal sounds. These are coupled with 160 non-vocal signals, gestures and

The Thunder Poet

expressions, but the most common communication method is the vocal call. These calls can be in the form of the typical trumpet call, a roar, a groan, a snort or a squeal, each with its own unique pitch of soft, shrill, low-pitched, or rumbling sounds. A burst of deafening blasts can also be emitted as an alarm, upon which members of the herd encircle the calves in a protective ring. Also vocal calls are commonly used by mothers when caring for their calves, during disagreements, or to rally members of the herd together for mass movements. Many of the sounds emitted by elephants are not audible to the human ear. The low-frequency sounds can be as deep as 1 to 20 Hz. At such a frequency, while not heard by the human ear, these sounds travel powerfully for miles. Such long-distance reach enables effective communication to distanced animals, whether for protection or mating or reuniting family groups.

    If an elephant is separated from his herd, the individual animal that desires to reunite with the other family members will emit a low rumble. This sound reverberates powerfully as it travels the surrounding area. Directly after making this sound, the elephant will raise its head to listen for a response. If a relative responds to this call, the elephant will sound an explosive noise. This pattern is then repeated until the elephants are reunited; it is a process that can last for hours. When the family members do eventually meet up, this occasion is marked by screaming, rumbling and the famous trumpet.

Still, the most fascinating thing about elephant communication is that each elephant has a unique "voice." This individual voice is recognizable to the hundreds of other elephants within a half-mile radius. His voice is his alone.[2]

God Delights in Singularity

Elephant vocal communication is just one example that undergirds the fact that God takes great delight in His one-of-a-kind masterpieces. The Psalmist prays praising God in Psalm 139:13-16, *"For it was You who created my inward parts; You knit me together in my mother's womb. I will praise You because I have been remarkably and wonderfully made. Your works are wonderful, and I know this very well. My bones were not hidden from You when I was made in secret, when I was formed in the depths of the earth. Your eyes saw me when I was formless; all my days were written in Your book and planned before a single one of them began."*

Do you understand what that means? Every tiny baby in its mother's womb is a product of God's pre-conceived plan. He designs the unique features of that tiny body in advance; and even pre-ordains the days and events of life in which that tiny person will live. He is very involved in details of the poems of our lives.

I am especially interested in that phrase, *"I have been remarkably and wonderfully made."* This phrase has the idea of an artist mixing his colors for a portrait, or a weaver weaving the fabric of a garment

The Thunder Poet

of cloth. In our mothers' wombs the Almighty was mixing the colors and weaving the fabric of our very existence. He chose the color of our hair and eyes. He chose the countenance of our face and the intricacies of our personalities. We are a work of the Master's hand.

God created us as He desired and He created us for a purpose. The physical attributes of our lives are only a portion of what God has created. He has also gifted us with particular abilities. Each of our lives was ordered from above. The Great Thunder Poet created us to become what He desired. But if we wish for our lives to rhyme with His indigenous design, we must willingly submit to His design. We must walk in obedience to His plan.

Sometimes in a big world with so much emphasis on big ideas and vast groups of people, we may be tempted to ask, "Does God genuinely care about me as an individual?" The revelation of God's Word is that He does! Perhaps our longing to know whether God cares is why so many people so easily connect with the book of Psalms in the Bible. Perhaps it is also why so many people spend so much of their personal quiet times in the Psalms. This great Bible book is one of the clearest pictures in God's Word of an individual intimately relating to God. Scripture reveals that the individual is very important to God.

When we consider the Biblical record of the ministry of Jesus while He was on earth, we find that many times He spoke to vast crowds and large groups of people, but many stories reveal when He spoke and had interactions with individuals only. The individual is obviously of great importance to God.

While the American brand of Christianity can focus and has often focused too much on the individual, the Kingdom is best represented when you as an individual are fully you, flourishing and growing in the place and with the gifts He has designed for you. He created you to be actually you. First Corinthians 12:27 tells us, *"Now <u>you</u> are the body of Christ, and <u>individual</u> members of it"* (Emphasis mine). God made each of us unique in many, many ways.

The "I Am Factor"

In his book, GOD IN THE MIRROR, Miles McPherson develops two concepts that help us to understand the importance of our uniqueness as individuals. First he talks about the "I Am Factor." Just as God is the great "I Am" in Scripture, He has created us in His image and shared a bit of that "I Am-ness" with each one of us. Interestingly, after God reveals Himself to Moses in the burning bush by the name, "I AM THAT I AM," Moses responds to God's call in his life by asking, *"<u>Who am I</u>, that I should go to the Pharaoh?"* (Exodus 3:11 emphasis mine). McPherson goes on to say that we reflect the "I Am-ness" of God like a diamond reflects light. "If you take a diamond into a room, no matter how many carets, no matter what the color of the diamond is, no matter how much brilliance it has, if you take that diamond into a dark room, you won't see anything. It needs external light to shine onto it and then it reflects that light back out. Our 'God image' is our spiritual diamond. It only has the ability to reflect God's glory back to Him. Each of us reflects God's glory back to Him in a very unique way."3

God Activated Uniqueness

God activates your uniqueness by empowering you with His Spirit to be the person that He created you to be. He shows you your purpose through Scripture, gives you the courage to be the person He created you to be, and then empowers you by His Spirit to live out the poem. The key is that you must be the person God designed. It is His design, not yours, that makes the difference. That is what is meant by "rhyming life with God's indigenous design." That's when you become the genuine you.

Do you know that according to Revelation 2:17, one day in eternity God is going to give you a white stone with your name on it and the only person other than the Almighty Himself who is going to know the name that is on that stone is the person to whom it is given? Are you interested to know that name? That name is going to reflect who you are by God's indigenous design. Is your life rhyming with that design?

I often speak of John the Baptist. I enjoy studying his life. He is one of my favorite characters in Scripture. Christ used him as an example of a man who truly had it altogether. He was a man who was consistent with the design God had created him to be.

Jesus said of him, *"I assure you: Among those born of women no one greater than John the Baptist has appeared . . ."* (Matthew 11:11). He was a rugged, virile, dynamic individual who reflected in his life the message that he had come to proclaim. His life rhymed with his purpose. We're told in Scripture that he wore a big leather belt wrapped around a roughed-out camel's hair garment and that he ate locusts and wild honey.

The honey, we like to think about. We think, "Hey! That's not too bad." Most everyone likes honey. It is smooth and sweet. Like jelly beans or Jolly Ranchers in our pockets on a long day of cross country hiking, we can easily imagine that honey made a delicious snack for John on a daily basis. But those locusts, well now that is different. A diet of locust? What does that mean? Historically, locusts have been associated with ravaging, land-stripping, crop-devouring pestilences. Often they devour all the vegetation in an area, leaving nothing behind. In that sense they are like sin and human dissipation that so easily devour human lives.

So What Does It Mean When John Eats Locusts?

Whenever John the Baptist ate those locusts, he performed and acted out a message consistent with the core of his existence. He was acting out a graphic line from the verses of his life poem. Every time he popped one of those crunchy creatures into his mouth, he was saying, "There is coming One Who will devour the devourer! There is coming One Who will reverse the process of Satan's curse and the results of man's tragic fall."

Is your life reflecting God's purpose for you and for you alone? Does your life rhyme with God's indigenous design?

Life's Most Important Response

Let me ask you a life-changing question here: What is the most important life response ever revealed in Scripture? What is the greatest challenge ever offered in God's Word? Jesus didn't leave us guessing. He said it is this: *"Love the Lord your God with all your heart, with all your soul, with all your mind, and with all your strength"* (Mark 12:30). Jesus said, "Nothing matters more than that. That's the number one thing in life. I want you to love Me passionately." Nothing else matters in life if you don't love God passionately. God doesn't want you to love Him half-heartedly. He wants all your heart, all your soul, all your mind, and all your strength.

When it comes to rhyming life with God's indigenous design, it is essential that we remember nothing great is ever accomplished without passion. NOTHING! Nothing great is ever sustained in life without passion. Passion is what energizes life. Passion describes a sold-out life. That is why Paul stresses in Romans 12:11, *"Never be lacking in zeal, but keep your spiritual fervor, serving the Lord"* (NIV).

Taylor

Hearts Like Hummingbirds

Spiritually speaking we should be like hummingbirds. Hummingbirds actually have hearts like race cars. Those hearts eat oxygen at a mind-boggling rate of more than 1,260 beats per minute. That compares to about 72 bpm in the average human adult, and only 20 bpm in the heart of a blue whale, the heart of which by itself weighs 1,000 pounds or more. Did you know some of the largest whales have had hearts that weigh 2,500 pounds—about the weight of a small car? In fact, a whale heart is about the size of a Volkswagen Beetle. A child could walk around in it head high, bending only to step through the valves. The valves are themselves as big as swinging doors on an old western saloon. And the whole creature (an adult whale) can weigh up to 150 tons with the largest ever recorded estimated to be 190 tons.

Compare that with a hummingbird. While it may be difficult for us to imagine, one type of hummingbird, the Bee Hummingbird, (Mellisuga helenae) is the smallest of all hummingbirds, and it weighs less than a penny or about the same as two paper clips. The heart of a hummingbird is usually about 2.5 percent of its total body weight. Can you imagine how tiny this little bird's heart must be? Amazingly tiny!

Hummingbirds are amazingly beautiful, too. Hummingbird colors are not produced by pigment, but rather by layers of air bubbles on their feathers. Even the fascinating names for

The Thunder Poet

hummingbirds in other parts of the world are beautiful—"Beija-Flor," which is Portuguese for "Flower-Kisser," and "Joyas Voladoras" which is Spanish for "Flying-Jewels."

While watching a National Geographic documentary recently, I discovered that every night of their lives hummingbirds face the challenge of staying alive until morning because of a deep sleep called "torpor." Torpor is a state of decreased physiological activity in an animal, usually by a reduced body temperature and metabolic rate. Somewhat like hibernation, torpor enables animals to survive periods of reduced food availability. It is a well-controlled thermo-regulatory process. The spokesman for the documentary described them as "every night living on the edge of what is possible" (National Geographic Wild channel).[4]

Hummingbirds beat their wings up to 80 times per second, but they do not actually flap their wings like other birds do. Instead they rotate them in figure eight patterns. This design allows them to fly in any direction.

Of course there is a price to pay to have the heart of a hummingbird. The price is a life always closer to death. They suffer more heart attacks, aneurysms, and vessel ruptures than any other creature. It is physically expensive to have a heart that beats at the rate theirs does—you burn out—you fry the machine—you melt the engine.[5]

The reason I'm sharing these statistics with you is because every creature on earth is born with a certain number of heartbeats. You can spend them slowly like the Giant Galapagos Tortoises who with a heart rate of only 4 beats per minute at rest can live to be 200 years old. On the other hand, you can spend them fast like a hummingbird and only live to be 2 to 5 years old.

Why would a person choose to live with such a passionate heart? <u>You get to fly</u>! And you get to fly in an amazing fashion—frontwards, backwards, sideways, hovering, and standing still. What a beautiful picture of a life-poem that rhymes!

When the Bible commands us, *"Never be lacking in zeal, but keep your spiritual fervor, serving the Lord"* (NIV), the word used for *"fervor"* is a verb that literally means, *"to be hot."* In reference to liquid it means *"to boil."* In reference to solids, it means *"to glow."* Thus it was used to describe boiling water or glowing metal. Figuratively the word was used to express spiritual fervor, eagerness, and enthusiasm.

"Business as usual" church and boring, mundane Christian living is the curse of American Christianity. This verse is a warning about settling into comfortable, shallow ruts in our spiritual lives.

Be careful that you understand what I am saying. The idea here is not that of being overheated to the point of boiling over and being out of control like charismatic frenzy. Rather it is to be like a steam engine that has sufficient heat to produce energy necessary to get the work done.

J. C. Ryle says, "Zeal in religion is a burning desire to please God, to do His will, and advance His glory in the world in every possible way."[6] Prior to being martyred at the hands of the Aucca Indians in South America, Jim Elliot wrote in his journal, "Wherever you are, be all there! Live to the hilt in every situation you believe to be the will of God."[7] Jonathan Edwards wrote as a young man in his famous 70 resolutions, "Resolved, to live with all my heart while I do live."[8] Paul is shouting in Romans 12:11, "the gospel ought to make your spirit boil!"

Interestingly, according to Paul's passage, such passion results in service. The problem with many believers is that they have never understood what Christian service is about. The Greek word for *"serve"* makes it clear. It means *"to be enslaved."* Since the Lord bought us out of the slave market of sin, we are not our own. We belong to Him as slaves belong to a Master. All that we are and all that we have is not ours, but His.

Do you understand what that enslavement means? Our time is not ours to use as we please. Our money is not ours to spend as we please. Our families are not ours to take priority over allegiance to the Lord. Our careers are not ours to pursue as we wish. Everything we have and are belongs to the Lord to be used for His glory and purpose.

A problem with American Christianity is that we have substituted the idea of "volunteerism" for ownership. There is a fundamental difference between slaves and volunteers. Volunteers choose when and how they serve; slaves are on call night and day. Volunteers can quit serving when they get tired; slaves are slaves for life. We belong to Christ and are owned by Him. The Master may adjust our duties along the way, but we are not free to quit.[9]

"Never be lacking in zeal, but keep your spiritual fervor, serving the Lord!" I like this translation of Romans 12:11. Circle that word, "keep." It's not automatic. It's a choice. It's something that you must maintain. It's something that you must choose to do. It has nothing to do with your personality or age. It's a matter of your will.

Wayne Cordeiro said in a sermon, "Life will not give you what you want, neither will it give you what you think you deserve. Life will give you what you are willing to settle for."[10]

The Bible uses some strong words to describe the opposite of a passionate man. One word is a *"sluggard."* Someone has described a sluggard as "an ordinary man who has made too many excuses."[11] Another word describes such a person's actions as *"laziness"*—"the tendency to remain where you are in life instead of moving to where you could be and should be."[12]

In 1761 a new hymnal came out with instructions for singing by John Wesley. It was thought that the instructions were needed because people were looking at the new hymns in that day with the same suspicion that people look at praise choruses of our generation. As result, they had stopped singing. Listen to instruction number # 4: "Sing with a good courage. Beware of singing as if you were half dead, or half asleep; but lift your voice up with strength." Then instruction number # 7: "Above all, sing spiritually. Have an eye to God in every word you sing. Aim at pleasing Him more than yourself or any other creature."[13]

The Thunder Poet

That last instruction reminds us of Phinehas in the Old Testament. He was a man who was known for his zeal for God's honor. Like instruction number #7, he aimed to please God more than himself or anyone else. *"Phinehas son of Eleazar, son of Aaron the priest, has turned back My wrath from the Israelites because he was zealous among them with My zeal, so that I did not destroy the Israelites in My zeal. Therefore declare: I grant him My covenant of peace. It will be a covenant of perpetual priesthood for him and his future descendants, because he was zealous for his God and made atonement for the Israelites"* (Numbers 25:11-13).

Our zeal should be noticeable and verifiable, too. Notice what is written about Jehu in 2 Kings 10:16, *"Then Jehu said, 'Come with me and see my zeal for the Lord!"* People ought to be able to see our zeal for the Lord.

Throughout Scripture the normal atmosphere for Christian ministry is spiritual energy and enthusiasm. I believe every preacher ought to preach as a pastor from the old days was described: when he preached—he preached "with logic on fire."[15] When you proclaim God's Word or serve before the Lord in any spiritual capacity, for that matter, you need to be intellectually sound and authentically literate with the authority of Scripture, but always with intensity and enthusiasm. To be successful you'll need the voice of an elephant and the heart of a hummingbird—a life marked by God's plan for uniqueness and passion.

Lion Hunters Selling Fudge

The year 2002 was a time of radical change in Zimbabwe. That year Robert Mugabe's plan for land redistribution was in full swing and hundreds of white farmers, conservationists, safari operators, and other land owners in Zimbabwe lost their land when it was confiscated by the Zimbabwean government. The lives of scores of these families were suddenly and thoroughly disrupted. Most of these people, having settled onto farms in the rural areas years before, now had to move into the cities to try and start their lives over again. Harare, Bulawayo, Gweru, Kwekwe, Masvingo, and Mutare grew rapidly with the sudden influx of these displaced people. Their lives and livelihoods were destroyed and jobs were non-existent in the new places to which they moved.

These rural refugees found survival difficult. Everything they had done to earn a living in the bush was taken away overnight. Many of them had to scramble and scrounge just to get by. They took odd jobs and part-time employment where that was an option. They sold wedding rings, and family jewelry, and their few remaining meager possessions for only a few cents on the dollar in an effort just to make ends meet.

Others tried to come up with creative ideas of income. Some took advantage of their mechanical skills and began to repair small engines and lawn and garden machines. Some dug up the backyards of their new city houses, and planted vegetable gardens to grow vegetables that they would take to the open air

The Thunder Poet

markets or try to sell on the street corners. Sometimes their wives would bake cookies and cakes—Vetkoeks and Koeksisters—some of the best of Afrikaans' pastries. These deserts made them especially popular as vendors on the corners. On rare occasions, when the ingredients were available, their wives would bake fudge. Fudge was even more popular with the buyers than the pastries, and it brought a premium price on the street corners and in the open-air markets.

At that time our work permits had been denied in Zimbabwe, so Shirley and I were living back in the states where I was pastoring a church in Albuquerque. When I heard news of what was going on, I called my dear friend and former safari hunter/conservationist Buck DeVries. As we spoke on the phone, he related the current conditions of land acquisition, vigilante violence, and unemployment among the safari hunting community. Finally, just before we hung up the phone, Buck concluded our conversation with his usual best wishes and greetings to my family. Then he said something that has stuck with me for years. He lamented the way things had become in Zimbabwe, the devastation of his way of life, and the loss of his freedom and income. Then he said this—pathetic words, an exclamation I'll never forget: *"No, Steve, can you believe it—<u>lion hunters selling fudge, just to get by</u>!"*

Those words sunk deep into my mind, and I found myself dwelling on them, thinking about them for days, and not just because of what they represent. Though Buck's comments represented the tragic ending of a way of life that I had observed and had admired for many years while living in Zimbabwe—the culmination of an era of history, the termination of a generation of adventurers, and the final closure of a culture that had sustained much of the effective wildlife conservation in Africa, I was also impressed by those words because they are such a concise description of what is sadly going on in many Christian lives in America today. Believers are called of God to represent Christ as Ambassadors in this world, to spread the gospel of our Most High Savior and Lord, to tear down strongholds of the evil one, to storm the gates of hell, and to advance the kingdom. We are "lion hunters" individually designed and uniquely commissioned to pursue, defeat, and overcome the great *"roaring lion who seeks to devour whom he may,"* rescuing from his grip those who have been *"held in slavery all their lives by fear of death."* Instead, many of us have devolved into petty clone-like passionless sellers of fudge. Instead of faithfully fulfilling the Great Commission of our Lord, seeking to advance the kingdom, and passionately working the works of the Father while it is yet day, we have developed all kinds of fudge-selling schemes—schemes that consume our time and that replace our effectiveness in global evangelism with busy work.

    Can you you imagine that? Lion hunters selling fudge just to get by! Plagiarized poems and passionless lives! These never rhyme with God's indigenous design.

Chapter 6

Nesting in a Shadow

> *"Poetry is an echo, asking a shadow to dance."*
> Carl Sandburg[1]

When the last light goes out in an African bush camp, the moon becomes a vandal. With a palette of dusky grays and murky blues, it paints lunar graffiti across the face of every flat surface. Silhouettes of the surroundings are intensified in the ashen light, and translucent canvas tent walls become make-shift projection screens for a temporary bush cinema magnifying the shape of every object. Backlit shadows of acacia thorns are transformed into javelins the size of whaling harpoons, and augmented reflections of grass stalks are exaggerated into giant swaying trees. Faraway in in a secluded place where fog settles late at night a baboon barks. The sound is louder than his voice, bizarrely amplified by resonating ricochets bouncing off the hardwood surfaces of mopane and teak trees. Like a banshee with a bullhorn, he screams out his raucous call producing a facsimile of cinematic surround-sound. Meanwhile I lie silent, motionless in a flimsy cloth shelter made of false security and fiber poles, cradled in a shallow bed of Kalahari sand, mesmerized by a private performance of God's midnight matinee.

    Those shadows on the tent wall were the Hollywood starlets of another world, a sometimes lonely world that existed for me as a young bush missionary while camping alone in the remote places of the Zambezi river Valley, a world today that features late-night replays rehashed in the memories of my mind. There were many nights during those early years when I fell asleep watching an original production, a drama of sorts, played out by vague apparitions of darkness. They were bigger than life characters, reflected overstated actors, theatrical forest personas, made of shade and subtlety, dancing in the night to the tune of a flickering fire.

    I could write an entire book on the shadows of Africa. I have observed them refined and polished beneath my feet, stark and black, sculpted by the focused aperture of a searing Zimbabwe sun. I have seen them turbid and undefined, lightly brushed and pastel painted by the blue-light of an African moon. I have even seen them without edges on moonless nights—borderless images of grizzled gray mysteriously sketched by expanding light rays of distant galactic stars.

The Thunder Poet

The Most Important Shadow—the Safest Place in the World

But the most important shadow I ever came to know during those years in Africa was the shadow of the Protector—God Almighty, Himself. David, a fellow wilderness dweller, lived under the influence of that shadow, too. He writes in Psalm 91:1, *"The one who lives under the protection of the Most High dwells in the shadow of the Almighty."* It is the Protector's shadow that we must come to understand and experience if we are to live out our lives rhyming with God's indigenous design.

Think for a moment of the safest place you've ever been. Some probably think of storm shelters. In south central Kansas where I live, those storm shelters offer a significant place of refuge. Sometimes huge towering black clouds build up in the southwest and generate tornadoes that can be so devastating that many people in our area have lost loved ones and property to those terrible storms. Others reading these words may think of panic rooms built into million dollar mansions as a hiding place from home invaders if the need should ever arise. Still others may think of caves, like those David found and in which he hid when running from King Saul—deep, dark, granite surrounded enclosures walled off entirely from the influences of the rest of the world.

Taylor

Lobengula's Cave

There is such a cave in the Manyanda area of Tongaland in northern Zimbabwe. A group of young Tonga men took me there once. The history that surrounds the cave is fascinating, and it involves one of the most famous of all the Matabele Kings—Lobengula, himself. "Historical enigmas that have remained unsolved in Zimbabwe don't get better than the disappearance of King Lobengula, whose remains have never been found. A British army—over 300 white soldiers and locals of an equal number—which was commanded by Major Allan Wilson had been wiped out at Pupu along the Shangani River in Lupane, buying the second and last Ndebele monarch time to evade capture. More troops were dispatched to bring in the king dead or alive, but because he had a head start, he was never captured. These caves are where King Lobengula was last seen. Tucked in a bushy area in Manyanda under Chief Pashu, what is now known as the Lobengula Caves has not been declared a national monument or explored by archeologists and history enthusiasts yet it is an integral part of the country's colonial history and a centre piece to the puzzle on King Lobengula's last chapter."[2] I stood at the entrance of these caves once, looking at their smooth river sand covered floors. I imagined how because of their remote locale, difficult access, and unfindable location, these must indeed be one of the safest hideouts in the world. However, Psalm 91 describes a safer place.

The Thunder Poet

To Whom the Shadow Belongs

We don't usually think of a shadow as a safe place for protection. But when that shadow belongs to the Most High—the Almighty God of all creation, a shadow is the safest place in the world. You see, the safety of a shadow depends entirely on whose shadow you're hiding in. The shadow of a Steenbuck, Zimbabwe's tiniest antelope, isn't a very safe place because he will flee away at the first sign of danger, but if you're a baby lion cub, hiding in your mama's shadow is one of the safest places you could ever be. It all depends to whom the shadow belongs.

Dwellers Only

The original meaning of the word translated *"dwells"* in the Psalmist's verse is a word that conveys the idea of wrapping oneself in a garment of warmth and rest during the cool of the night. The reflexive verb form is used here, so it actually means, *"The one who lives under the protection of the Most High shall wrap himself up in the shadow of the God of All Might."* "Intimacy with God is pictured here like a traveler who wraps a garment around himself as he goes to sleep in the desert, when the chills of night descend." God's intimate presence is to be wrapped around us for our protection.[3] The safest place in the world is in intimate fellowship with God.

That deep communion is why the emphasis of God's Word is that these promises are reserved for "abiders," for "dwellers;" not for "visitors" or "occasional guests." If you refuse to dwell in the shadow of the Almighty, you have no reasonable basis to expect that these promises of protection are for you. These promises are not for those who only occasionally visit the Lord or for those who run to God only in times of trouble. These promises are for those who passionately long for time alone with God. Vance Havner said, "We cannot rest in God until we nest in God. To nest is to settle, to abide."[4]

The essential thing is nearness of the soul to God. Show me a person with deep faith in God and I'll show you a person who has spent much time alone with God. P. T. Forsyth warned of the dangers of being religious without spiritual intimacy with God. "In that condition a person becomes satisfied even when no spiritual growth occurs in his life. His faith operates only on level ground. It does not mount up *"with wings like eagles"* and it never soars. New vistas of faith never rise before his soul. God becomes a habit for such an individual but He is no longer a habitation. With a person like that, God is not denied, but He is disregarded, taken for granted like the air and the sky."[5]

Reciprocal Intimacy

T. H. Darlow described Psalm 91 as "the Beatitude of the Inner Circle."[6] What that means is that this is a psalm especially for those who want to be intimately close to Christ. Some people are actually surprised to discover that there are differing levels of closeness among believers when it comes to a

The Thunder Poet

relationship with Christ, but it should not surprise us as we examine the narratives of the New Testament. Jesus had a special place in His heart for those who wanted the deep relationship of a sold-out follower. Even among His chosen twelve He had an inner circle of three who showed extraordinary passion to be near Him.

In James 4:8, the Apostle James reminds us to *"Draw near to God and He will draw near to you."* I like to describe that concept as <u>reciprocal intimacy</u>. As we draw nearer to Him, He draws nearer to us. The key to God's abiding presence in your life is abiding continually in Him, and the benefit of that continuous abiding is that you will discover that He delights in reminding you of His presence. Sometimes it is like a lover who shares a note with the one loved or a faithful friend who shares a card with the one who is the object of his affection. In a similar way He blesses us with the encouragement of His reciprocal intimacy by sending us reminders of His continual presence in the midst of the experiences of life as we seek to pursue His will.

The Bolt

A couple of years ago I had a large group of volunteers who went along with me on our annual Rock Cry Expedition to the Zambezi River Valley. This particular group was made up of all young men (except for yours truly, that is), and I chose as our destination some incredibly remote places. Among those places was the secluded village of Simatelele.

Because of the size of our group, I had sent Mufundisi Canann Kawina ahead to make preparations for our arrival—a two day trek from where we had met up with him at a place called Mumpande. Since our vehicle was completely full of expedition team members, I had to pull a trailer containing all of our ministry and camping supplies. We were riding in a big F 250 Ford with a stretch cab and an elevated seat mounted high above the truck bed—a superb elephant hunting vehicle belonging to a friend in Bulawayo. We left the main road and made our way toward Simatelele. The extremely rough roads of the Zambezi Valley take their toll on both vehicle and trailer as well as the human bodies of passengers who suffer a constant pounding. The route to our destination required that we skirt a mountain in a horseshoe pattern that would finally arrive at our destination. As we traveled along someone shouted, *"Our trailer is leaning badly to the left!"* By this time we were on the backside of the mountain within 20 kilometers of our destination, but we had no choice. We had to stop and investigate the problem. When we did, it was quickly assessed that a bolt attaching the leaf springs to the trailer had fallen off and we had lost it somewhere on the dust road over the course of the many rough miles we had traveled. We desperately needed to recover it since there was no source of replacement for many miles and no hope of progress until it was replaced.

  As always, I had to quickly make a plan. I disconnected the trailer and left a small group of our team with it because all of our supplies were on board, and it was essential for us to protect them. I sent a

The Thunder Poet

second group of our team—the younger guys—in a group of three walking on the road, backtracking the direction from where we had come. They were to carefully scour every square inch of the road in an attempt to locate the bolt in the area as far as they could travel by foot. In the meantime I took three other guys with me in the truck—one in the front seat opposite from me and two in the bed of the truck. The plan was that the two of us in front would look ahead for the bolt as I drove along slowly and carefully, while the guys in the back would search the road on each of the sides. The search continued for 15 kilometers. Finally I decided we had gone far enough to compensate for where the bolt could have possibly fallen out, so I decided to turn around and head back toward the rest of the team.

We had been unsuccessful. Finding that bolt on a 15 kilometer stretch of a dust covered road was a nearly impossible task. Those dust roads of Zimbabwe are extremely cramped, so I had to swing wide in order to make a U-turn. Just then a shout came from the back, *"Watch out for that sharp rock!"* It was too late. Pssssssh! The tire was punctured. Normally, this would have been no problem. After all, we have two spares and our high-lift jack in the trailer and another spare bolted to the backside of the truck. *"Wait a minute? <u>In the trailer!</u>"* We were 15 kilometers from the trailer with no jack, and our team was divided into three groups – two guys sitting with the trailer, three guys walking on the road 10 kilometers behind us, and the rest of us stuck with a flat and no jack.

Once again we were in what the Tongas call a *"mapickel." "Not sure how we're going to get out of this one."*

We did the only thing we could do. We started to pray. After we had prayed, I did what I always do ever since cell towers have been installed in the Zambezi Valley for tourists to use while fishing for Tiger Fish at Binga and when I find myself in one of those "no-way-out situations." I called my wife Shirley back in the states and told her to please form a prayer team. I also asked her to try and call Mufundisi Canaan Kawina who was on the backside of the mountain that separated us now. I asked her to tell him that I might be late or perhaps not make it at all for tonight's evangelism meeting.

It was at this point that the hand of God began to move in our lives as by His grace He desired to remind us of His unceasing presence with us. The shadow of His presence fell across our lives in the midst of a horrendous situation and He proved Himself true to His word—*"And lo, I am with you always, even to the ends of the earth"* (Matthew 28: KJV). Unknown to us at the time, two kilometers beyond where we were stranded, our Tonga evangelism/praise team was walking from Mumpande toward us. They had crossed the rivers and mountains on foot between where we were and where they started in order to be with us for our meeting that night. Their shortcut had joined the dust road near where we were waiting. Twenty minutes later they were coming down the hill that

The Thunder Poet

was 400 meters behind us on the road. We could see them as they made their approach.

When they arrived at our location, I explained our dilemma. They whispered to one another in ChiTonga and then flashed big smiles in my direction. I understood what they were about to do, so I got the tire tool that fortunately was located under the driver's seat and began to loosen the lug nuts. Thirteen strong Tonga young men with awesome voices that rival the roar of the booming waters of Victoria Falls and with willing strength that causes this missionary to marvel, backed up to the truck and together lifted with their legs. They held a heavy duty F-250 Ford truck in place while I changed the tire. At the same time a Red Cross relief truck was making its way out of the bush from the direction of our trailer—the only vehicle we saw on that road in two days—and the driver had stopped for our three young men walking and then later for Mufundisi Canaan Kawina whom Shirley had been able to contact by cell phone, though she could no longer contact me, and who "by chance" had started out on a random path from Simatelele across the mountain that separated us, in hopes of intersecting us on the road. Amazingly, considering all the points he could have stepped out of the bush onto the road along that 15 kilometer stretch, beyond the trailer or behind us, the one place that he stepped out was a place of providence. With his first step onto the road, he stepped on something hard and unnatural. He bent down to pick it up and recovered the bolt we all had been searching for. Soon we were all reunited, but our conversation for the rest of the night focused only on one thing—the awesome presence of God in the midst of all the situations of our lives. *"Draw near to God and He will draw near to you."* And when you do, you'll find yourself standing in the shadow of His presence.

His Presence is His Provision

When we draw near to God, He not only reveals His presence, but He also provides for those who draw near to Him. *"The one who lives under the protection of the Most High dwells in the <u>shadow</u> of the Almighty."*

An Example from the Tabernacle

An example of this is found in Exodus 26. In verse 14, while God was giving Moses instructions for building the tabernacle, we read, *"Make for the tent a covering of ram's skin dyed red and over that a covering of hides of sea cows."*

God's instructions for building the tabernacle are specific and precise. The reason for this precision is clear. This is important because according to the Word of God everything in the tabernacle points to Jesus Christ, every bit of building material, every item of furniture, every piece of cloth, every dimension, and every ornament in it are of extreme significance. This is because every single aspect of the tabernacle was a testimony to our Lord Jesus Christ.

Construction of roof is no exception to that rule. There were to be four consecutive layers of cloth

The Thunder Poet

and weather-proof leather. Let's consider each of them.

Beginning from the inside out, the first layer was to be the innermost decorative ceiling. It was made of white linen embroidered with purple, red, and blue. This elaborately embroidered linen ceiling represents Christ—His royalty, His sacrifice, and His righteousness.

The next layer was made of goat's hair. This layer of goat's hair reminds us that like the scape goat of the Old Testament, Christ took our sin upon Himself.

The third layer was to be made of ram's hide died red. The crimson red color brings to mind the shed blood of Jesus Who took our place. The substitutionary provision of His sacrificial death is foreshadowed in the ram caught in thicket that took Isaac's place in Genesis 22.

The final layer of the roof was to be made from the hides of sea cows. It is true that the King James Version translates this verse as *"badger's skins,"* but the original Hebrew word is clearly the word for the hides of "sea cows." It refers to a marine animal, a sea animal that teemed abundantly in the Nile River and Red Sea. The technical name for this animal is the "dugong." The dugong is an animal much like the Florida manatee.

During ancient days of the time of wandering in the wilderness for the children of Israel, it was common knowledge that the hide from the dugong made excellent leather. It was leather that was impervious to weather. In fact when this leather becomes dry, it becomes as hard as stone. The Beja tribesmen of Sudan still make their battle shields from it, and as far back as the time of the Israelites, it was considered the very best leather for making shoes. Even today, in parts of Europe, shoes are made from this leather.

Our English word "pachyderm" means "thick skin." Animals included in this category are the elephants, the rhinoceroses, and the hippos. Because of their thick skin, some scientists insist on including these sea cows in this category as well. It was from this material that the outer covering to the tabernacle was made.

How Does this Apply to the Provision of God's Presence?

If you and I are ever going to make a significant impact on the world for glory of Christ, if we are going to find the poetic rhyme of God's indigenous design for our life, we must demonstrate that we believe enough in His presence and provision that we are willing to sacrifice whatever it takes to accomplish this task in our world.

To understand this provision we need to ask a question—where did these sea cow hides come from in the first place? We've already seen that sea cows teemed abundantly in Red Sea and Nile River, but where could these animals possibly be found in the desert? Apparently, the Israelites had stocked up on an abundant supply of these hides prior to their departure. They likely had done so for a good reason.

The Thunder Poet

Prior to their departure, they prepared for a journey where they were to pass through rough and rocky desert. A supply of shoe making material had to be gathered. Sea cow leather was the material of choice from which these durable and much needed shoes would be made. No doubt they had brought these skins for shoe leather. Now the Lord was demanding that they give it up. He was asking them to demonstrate both trust in His presence and faith in His provision by giving up precious material that was abundant in Egypt but totally unavailable in the desert. He was literally asking them to give the shoes off their feet for the sake of His purpose and the rhyme of His poem.

At first, this sacrifice no doubt seemed like an unreasonable demand. Yet God had in mind for them a life of supernatural living. He was composing a poem, the rhyme of which they could not understand. When you and I begin to value God's purpose so much that we are willing to give of ourselves freely to see its accomplishment in our world, we will discover that our safety, our success, our reputation, our protection and our provision are all completely in His hands. If we are faithful to God's purpose, He will faithfully provide for us. Our lives will fruitfully rhyme with God's indigenous design.

That's the lesson the Israelites had to learn and a lesson we need to learn, too. It was as if God was saying, *"You give Me your shoe leather and I'll take care of your feet."* And He did just that. Forty years passed, but in Deuteronomy 29:5 He says, *"During the forty years I led you through the desert your* *clothes did not wear out, <u>nor did the sandals on your feet</u>"* (Emphasis mine). God said, *"You give me your shoe leather, and I'll give you something better. I'll give you shoes that won't wear out."* The longevity of their shoes is a testimony of God's provision for those who put His priorities first. *"Draw near to God and He will draw near to you."* <u>It is reciprocal intimacy</u>. *"The one who lives under the protection of the Most High dwells in the <u>shadow</u> of the Almighty."*

Nearness to God

Some translations of Scripture translate *"the <u>protection</u> of God"* as His *"secret place."* We read *"He who dwells in the secret place of the Most High shall abide under the shadow of the Almighty"* (King James Version 2000 Bible). The *"secret place"* in the Old Testament was the *"Holy of Holies"*—the mystic abiding place of the eternal God. In the Holy of Holies there was the Ark of the Covenant. On top of the Ark was a slab of gold called *"the mercy seat."* On either side of that mercy seat were the cherubim with wings outstretched across it. That mercy seat was the center of the mysterious presence of God. Today, because of the redeeming work of Christ, the secret place is not limited to a particular locality, it means nearness to God.

Nearness to God is what is symbolized by the arrangements of the temple. There was the outer court and the inner court, the holy place and the most holy place—each location symbolizing an increasing nearness to the heart of God. Life can be all "outside"

The Thunder Poet

for a believer. It can be like spending the entirety of its duration in the "outer courts." Life described like that for a believer is life that is experienced on the mere fringe of being. Life like that never rhymes, nor can it ever be life in the "secret place" where all meaning is found in fellowship and nearness to God. That is the primary meaning of life in the "secret place." It is life abandoning the mere outside of things, refusing to dwell in the outer halls.

The Vestibule of Heaven

One of the most meaningful descriptions of this intimacy that I ever came across in my lifetime was given to me by a dear friend during a time of tremendous need for an understanding of the importance of nearness to God. It is found in the form of a tract by G. D. Watson entitled, OTHERS MAY, YOU CANNOT. Since it is in the form of a common tract, some never pause to consider the depth of its meaning or to consider how profound a document it is. It is, however, without a doubt one of the best descriptions of intimacy with God and discovery of the secret place of His dwelling that I have ever come across. Because of its significance for me and its eternal impact on the direction of my life, I quote it in its entirety for you here:

> *If God has called you to be really like Jesus, He will draw you into a life of crucifixion and humility, and put upon you such demands of obedience,*

that you will not be able to follow other people, or measure yourself by other Christians, and in many ways He will seem to let other good people do things which He will not let you do.

Other Christians and ministers who seem very religious and useful, may push themselves, pull wires, and work schemes to carry out their plans, but you cannot do it; and if you attempt it, you will meet with such failure and rebuke from the Lord as to make you sorely penitent.

Others may boast of themselves, of their work, of their success, of their writings, but the Holy Spirit will not allow you to do any such thing, and if you begin it, He will lead you into some deep mortification that will make you despise yourself and all your good works.

Others may be allowed to succeed in making money, or may have a legacy left to them, but it is likely God will keep you poor, because He wants you to have something far better than gold, namely, a helpless dependence on Him, that He may have the privilege of supplying your needs day by day out of an unseen treasury.

The Lord may let others be honored and put forward, and keep you

The Thunder Poet

hidden in obscurity, because He wants you to produce some choice, fragrant fruit for His coming glory, which can only be produced in the shade. He may let others be great, but keep you small. He may let others do a work for Him and get the credit for it, but He will make you work and toil on without knowing how much you are doing; and then to make your work still more precious, He may let others get the credit for the work which you have done, and thus make your reward ten times greater when Jesus comes.

The Holy Spirit will put a strict watch over you, with a jealous love, and will rebuke you for little words and feelings, or for wasting your time, which other Christians never seem distressed over. So make up your mind that God is an infinite Sovereign, and has a right to do as He pleases with His own. He may not explain to you a thousand things which puzzle your reason in His dealings with you, but if you absolutely sell yourself to be His love slave, He will wrap you up in a jealous love, and bestow upon you many blessings which come only to those who are in the inner circle.

Settle it forever, then, that you are to deal directly with the Holy Spirit, and that He is to have the privilege of tying your tongue, or chaining your hand, or closing your eyes, in ways that He does not seem to use with others. Now when you are so possessed with the loving God that you are, in your secret heart, pleased and delighted over this peculiar, personal, private, jealous guardianship and management of the Holy Spirit over your life, you will have found the vestibule of Heaven.[7]

The Psalm of Protection

Psalm 91 is often referred to as "the Psalm of protection." The safest place in the world is in fellowship with God. That is a place of protection. One of the great privileges of the faithful child of God is the protection afforded to him from dwelling in the presence of the Most High. First Peter 1:5 describes that protection, *"You are being protected by God's power through faith for a salvation that is ready to be revealed in the last time."* The word translated *"protected"* is taken from a word that means *"sentinel."* It means *"to maintain a watch over"* or *"to guard."* That verb in this verse is in the present tense which means it represents continual protection. We are constantly being kept guarded by the power of God.

There is a story of an old Scotsman who was typically tight economically speaking. Before he died he left instructions that only one word should be engraved on his tombstone—the single word was the word "kept."[8] That is a beautiful one word description of the protection of God.

My favorite quote from David Livingstone is "I am immortal until God's will for me on earth has been accomplished."[9] God's protection is with faithful believers who dwell in the secret place and the shadow of His presence.

On either side of the mercy seat were <u>angels</u>. Interestingly verse 11 of Psalm 91 tells us clearly, *"For He will give His <u>angels</u> orders concerning you, to protect you in all your ways."* As we have seen above in the 1 Peter passage the term *"protected"* is a military term. That implies that those who are born again are under enemy attack, but we are surrounded by a garrison of troops conducting us with safe passage to the place where our eternal inheritance awaits us. As believers we need to be certain we keep our theology straight in line with Scripture when it comes to angels, but we also need to realize that God uses these ministering agents to protect us along our way.

Buffalo or Angels?

As I mentioned in the previous chapter, 2002 was a politically volatile flashpoint year in Zimbabwe. Conflict over land acquisition and redistribution had become a manipulative tool in the hand of Zimbabwe's dictator, Robert Mugabe. Under the guise of redistributing land to needy peasants and villagers, Mugabe re-established and undergirded his political strength by taking land from productive white ranchers, farmers, and conservationists, and giving it to his bureaucratic cronies. Hundreds of white Zimbabwean families lost everything overnight—housing, possessions, and land.

    The time leading up to the land takeover was turbulent and violent, and many innocent lives were lost. Rule by lawless intimidation was widespread as armed war vets and bandits roamed throughout the country. Food supplies were difficult if not impossible to come by, and transported truckloads of food were often confiscated on Zimbabwe's roads at the point of a gun.

    As I also mentioned in the previous chapter, Shirley and I were back in the USA at the time, living in Albuquerque, New Mexico, but as always, I made my annual mission trek back to the Zambezi River Valley. In those years Rock Cry Expeditions was in its infancy, and at that time we did not have a waiting list of mission volunteers looking for a chance to be a part of a dangerous and potentially violent trip. One young associate pastor with a heart burning for adventure and full of the reckless courage of youth had come along with me that year. He had sensed that the Lord was leading him to risk it all for the sake of others.

    I had arranged for a big lorry (truck) full of mealie meal in order to take food relief out to starving villages of people in the valley. We loaded the truck from a hidden stash that a friend of mine had collected on his conservancy in a remote and secluded place in the bush. We arranged that a driver, a fearless young African man, would deliver the food at a

The Thunder Poet

specified village in the valley at 2:00 AM. Our hope was that this "middle of the night" delivery would prevent the supplies from being stolen by bandits along the way.

The young associate and I drove ahead earlier in a Land Rover and made arrangements at the village for the distribution of the food. Our plan was to drive back to my friend's conservancy after the food was delivered where we would camp in the relative safety of the isolated game-rich location. Facing a choice, I have always preferred to take my chances sleeping among the wild animals over trying to sleep with bandits in the area.

We were driving through the Dete Vlei in the darkness of the early morning hours, having left the large truck at the bush village to return during the daylight of the next day. A layer of cobalt fog hung inches above the ground stretching flat into the gloom as far as I could see. A bright stalking moon bleached the fog leaden gray at the top, level and heavy looking, bizarre like the deck of a battleship moored in a swamp. A small group of elephants moved silently through the mist like islands moving through the sea, the only sound—my diesel clacking like a 50 mm projector in a cavern.

Ahead in the lights I saw the distinct shape of men standing shoulder to shoulder, blocking the path of the trail to our destination. There were three of them, each with an AK47 in his hand. Memories of a previous armed robbery flashed through my mind. As I instinctually reached down with my left hand to downshift the gear I determined I would not stop.

Sliding into second gear and accelerating simultaneously, I pulled hard to the right running into the Vlei to avoid the men. I shouted to my young associate to get His head down in case the men started shooting. No gunfire sounded as we sped away into the night. But then I began to ponder another thought with dread. All those men would have to do is follow the tracks of our tires to where we were sleeping. They could rob us at will from that advantage while we slept.

It was then that we saw the hand of God moving once again in our lives. Out of both sides of the bush, a herd of Cape buffalo, hundreds strong, began to surround us from every side. They began to completely engulf the Land Rover and I had to bring its progress to a snail's pace as I moved slowly through the herd for more than a mile. Finally we made our way through to the other side.

From there we traveled on to where we had set up our camp the previous day. It was a futile attempt at a couple of hours of fitful sleep before the sun came up bringing light and comfort. It's amazing how much safer the daytime can make us feel.

After a strong breakfast of Vienna sausages and peanut butter logs, we made our way back to where we had encountered the men a few hours before. The tracks and the spoor told the whole story. As I had supposed, the men had followed our tracks until they came to the place where the buffalo were. From that point they made a U-turn and retreated to the direction from which they had come. The pounding hoofs of the buffalo had completely covered and

The Thunder Poet

erased our tracks. There was no way they could have found us.

"For He will give His <u>angels</u> orders concerning you, to protect you in all your ways." "The one who lives under the protection of the Most High dwells in the <u>shadow</u> of the Almighty."

Days later when I returned home and told Shirley the story, she had only one question for me, "Do you think those were buffaloes or angels?" I cannot say with certainty what they were, but I can tell you this—they were God's agents of protection and provision for me on a dark and scary night on the Dete Vlei. If life is going to rhyme with God's indigenous design, we must move in so closely to Him that we nest in His shadow. In that nearness the protection of His shadow falls across us, guarding the pathway of the poem He has written for our lives.

Chapter 7

A Log Left Burning in an African Campfire

"Perish the thought that ash be ash and not the memory of an ember."
Erin Hanson[1]

Chief Kafula's royal kraal is located south of Lubimbi near the village of Kamambo. It is situated on the pinnacle of a high hill separated from the nearby Chimeja Mountains by deep broken ravines. It overlooks rugged brushy hills covered with a thick bush of Zambezi River Valley undergrowth and huge virgin forests of teak and mahogany trees. Giant baobab trees are scattered through the forests like colossal corner posts that support endless green fence rows running in every direction.

I was seated in the meager shade of a musassa tree on a rustic Tonga stool carved from mukamba wood. I leaned back against a large grey granite rock that formed a perfect back rest for the occasion. Chief Kafula was seated across from me reclining on the narrow seat of a traditional slatted Tonga chair, seeking a place of shaded comfort made by the shadow of his hut as the sun sank deeper on a late summer afternoon. His face was illuminated by the gilded glow of a growing sunset, the yellow taupe particles of sand highlighted against his ebony skin like gold dust shining in an exaggerated three-dimensional fashion. The clarity of the moment reminded me of an early childhood memory—my first look at scenes of nature through a viewfinder.

He wore a dingy "un-kingly" u-shirt, and his lips encased a wide smile with large teeth the color of Neolithic amber. All the semblance of eggshells had been tarnished by discoloring many years before.

We were surrounded by an entourage made up of a majority of young men—relatives of the chief mainly—sons and nephews who were curious to meet the chief's mukuwa guest. The young men who accompanied me, though sharing no blood relation and bearing no family resemblance, were nonetheless my true sons in the faith—relationships that had developed over many years of working with them in the Zambezi Valley.

Small talk was in order at first. As usual, greetings were exchanged all around. Each person in Tonga culture is acknowledged as someone significant. Even a young teenage girl standing in the doorway behind the chief was recognized as important, though when I greeted her she responded with the typical humility of a well-tutored Tonga girl, "Changwe?" "Why are you even noticing me?"

The Thunder Poet

The tone of the conversation that day was relaxed but inquisitive. The chief seemed interested in how I had first come to Tongaland, why I had chosen this valley of all the places in the world, and what my plans were for the future of the work. Canann Kawina interjected comments and details about the success of the work—how lives had been changed and how many churches had been started among the Tonga people. He related how I had come to live among the Tonga people, how I had been given a ChiTonga name, (Musungwaazi Munsaka), and how I had personally baptized each of the young men seated there. We enjoyed an afternoon of memories and reflection as Canann continued to relate stories of our remote camping expeditions and vehicle break-downs in the deep bush during those early days, of my close friendship with Canann's father Jacob who is no longer living in this world, of my relationship with the old Chief Saba and Chief Pashu, of long hikes, of snake-killing adventures, of mountain climbing, river crossings, run-ins with hippos and crocodiles, of being lost in the bush on dark nights, and of my learning to eat termites after catching them in flight and crunching them quickly before they could move in my mouth. He shared about the values I had taught, Biblical truths, life lessons and deep convictions of my heart—the all-sufficient atoning work of Jesus Christ on the cross, the integrity and perfect trustworthiness of the Word of God, and the responsibility of every believer to make a sold-out, personal, and passionate response with his life committed to the Lord.

By the time Canann finished relating the stories, the sun was sinking low over the northwest corner of the Chimejas, and with hands clapping lightly and fingers pointing forward we stood to take our leave. At that moment just to my left, a young man, one of the chief's nephews, stood to his feet and with a beaming smile and an affirming voice he spoke softly and said, *"Mweenzu usiya chisisi."* That is an old Tonga proverb, and it means, *"When a visitor departs, he leaves a log burning in the campfire."* I realized in that instant that Canann had just recited my legacy among the Tongas. Regardless of where I go in this world and regardless of what may happen in the future, I have left a "log burning in the campfire" there in the Zambezi River Valley. That "burning log" is a major part of the legacy of my life.

What does it Mean to Leave a Legacy?

Simply put, leaving a legacy means that you leave something behind for those who remain after you die. It means that you leave something in the wake of your life that lives on even after you are gone. One of the best descriptions of legacy that I ever came across is—"Legacy is the residue of a life well-lived."[2] If life is going to rhyme with God's indigenous design, we must choose to live life in such a way that what we teach, how we serve, when we influence others with our life here on earth, and where the impact of our living for the glory of God's call, all line up with God's intended plan.

The Thunder Poet

"What Will Your Verse Be?"

The Dead Poets Society is an American film set in 1959 at a fictional elite conservative boarding school located in Vermont. The film starred Robin Williams as John Keating, an English teacher who inspires his students through his teaching of poetry. In one scene, Keating talks to his students about the meaning of life; then he quotes from Walt Whitman's poem, *"O Me! O Life!"* The poem essentially asks a question regarding the meaning of life. Then a line from Whitman's poem answers that question in this way:

> "That you are here—that life exists and identity, that the powerful play goes on, and you may contribute a verse."

The poem explains that life is like a play, in which everyone who has ever lived gets to contribute a verse. Keating then asks the students: "What will your verse be?"[3] The verse that you contribute to the play of life is your legacy. That's your log left burning in the campfire.

The Generational Bounce

There is a great Old Testament passage in Psalm 145:4 that tells us, *"One generation will declare Your works to the next and will proclaim Your mighty acts."* It is the solemn duty of every generation to tell to the next generation the story of what God has done for them, and to tell it well. To fail to do this faithfully is to rob the future of the treasures of the past. In fact, every generation stands at the crossroad of history. We are a link in between the past and the future. We cannot afford to be indifferent about this. The Hebrew word used in this verse for *"proclaim"* is spectacular. It means *"to shout in triumph"* and carries with it the idea of loud, vocal, public praise full of volume and zeal. "If we can recount the miracles we have seen as if we were reading the recipe for tuna casserole, then something is badly wrong with us. And the great danger is, our children will get the idea that God is boring and doesn't matter."[4]

Dry, unemotional, indifferent teaching about God or half-hearted lukewarm living for God is a disgrace at best, and at worst it is a travesty of shameful sinfulness that will have devastating effects on future generations. Looking at it from the perspective of a future generation, legacy is what someone has left behind and what someone currently living can benefit from.

I like the way Carl Jernigan describes it. He says, "It's the 'jump' or the 'bounce' you get in life from someone else's energy. Think of yourself as standing on a trampoline. Someone puts the energy into jumping and you get propelled. It is not because you 'did anything' but because they did and they directed their energy and efforts toward you!"[5] That's what it means to leave a legacy and to benefit from one.

The Thunder Poet

Legacy is Like a Pointer

Whenever I camp in the Southern Hemisphere I always feel at home. Years of camping night after night, week after week, month after month in the same sand, hanging from the same trees, surrounded by the same night sounds, looking at the same Zimbabwean night sky has created a comforting familiarity that I feel in no other location. A view of the Southern Cross while hanging in my hammock on the first night of each year's expedition brings the satisfaction and solace of a wanderer returned.

The Southern Cross is one of the most recognizable patterns of stars in the southern night sky and forms part of the constellation Crux. The Cross itself is actually classed as an asterism, not a constellation, as the word "constellation" is reserved as a reference to 88 specific areas of the whole night sky. The Southern Cross is the Southern Hemisphere equivalent to the Big Dipper and North Star of the Northern Hemisphere, and it is key to determining direction since it is always possible to ascertain a southern direction by consulting it.

The Southern Cross is made up of the four brightest stars within the constellation Crux but it can sometimes be confused with another nearby asterism called the False Cross—part of the constellation Vela. The easiest way to be sure you've found the Southern Cross is to look for the two bright pointer stars that always point to it.

These pointers are Alpha Centauri, a bright white star, and Beta Centauri, a blue-white star. They form a straight line of pointers on the right side of the Cross continually pointing to the asterism and assisting the observer with its location.[6] In that sense the importance of these pointers cannot be overstated. Without their existence, locating the Cross would be much more challenging. They make it possible to site one of the most important star patterns in the African sky.

The legacy of life is like that, too. The purpose of legacy is to point with our lives to One Who gives direction, meter, rhyme, and significance to the poem of every believer's life. Legacy gives meaning to our being.

Mentors and Mentees

Leaving a legacy is about the relationship that exists between a mentor and the one being mentored. According to Homer's *Odyssey*, when King Odysseus went off to fight in the Trojan War, he left his son Telemachus in the hands of a wise old man named Mentor. Mentor was charged with the task of teaching the young man wisdom. More than 2,000 years after Homer, a French scholar and theologian by the name of François Fénelon adapted the story of Telemachus in a novel titled TE'LE'MAQUE. In it he enlarged the character of Mentor. The word "mentor" soon came to mean "a wise and responsible tutor"—an experienced person who advises, guides, teaches, inspires, challenges, corrects, and serves as a model.[7]

The Thunder Poet

The mentor/mentee relationship is the relationship that the psalmist describes in Psalm 145:4. It is a vital relationship when it comes to leaving a legacy. *"One generation will declare Your works to the next and will proclaim Your mighty acts."* It is the key to the poignancy of the challenge of Ayesha Saddiqui's famous quote, "Be the person you needed when you were younger."[8]

The *Merriam-Webster Dictionary* defines "mentor" as a trusted counselor or guide. A mentor is an individual, usually older, always more experienced, who helps guide another individual's development. The mentor's role is to guide, to give advice, and to support the mentee. A mentor can help a person improve his or her abilities and skills through observation, assessment, modeling, and by providing guidance.[9] This relationship is an essential ingredient for leaving a legacy.

A Priority Responsibility

Second Timothy 2:2 is also a passage that speaks specifically to the subject of leaving a legacy. *"And what you have heard from me in the presence of many witnesses, commit to faithful men who will be able to teach others also."* Four generations are listed in this text—Paul, Timothy, faithful men, and others they may teach also. This verse indicates that leaving a legacy is one of the most important responsibilities in the believer's life.

The word *"commit"* in this passage is translated from the Greek word, *"paratithemi."* That word is a compound verb formed from two other words – *"para"* meaning *"beside"* and *"tithemi"* meaning *"to place."* This verb conveys the idea of placing a precious treasure into the hands of another person for the purpose of safekeeping. Figuratively we sometimes describe this process as "pouring one's life into another person." In the secular Greco-Roman world, *"paratithemi"* was used as a banking term meaning to deposit something valuable as a trust or for protection. The point of this specific verb is that truth is not simply to be given away, but is to be carefully deposited. Again the picture of a relay race comes to mind. The baton must be safely passed from one runner to another.[10]

An Entrusted Treasure

To whom is the treasure entrusted? The Bible says the treasure is to be committed to *"faithful men."* These *"faithful men"* are to be loyal and reliable believers. And what is the primary characteristic of these *"faithful men?"* They are men who can be trusted as reliable to maintain the standard of sound doctrine and who can be counted on to be dependable in fulfilling the ministry that has been entrusted to them. Long ago as a pastor and as a missionary I learned the value of entrusting the gospel and the ministry to *"faithful"* men. We can never underestimate the power of passing on the Word of God to *trustworthy* people. This transmission is vital to legacy.

The Thunder Poet

The word *"faithful"* translates from the Greek word *"pistos,"* meaning *"convinced"* or *"persuaded,"* and describes someone who is worthy of our faith or who keeps his promises. It refers to a person who is reliable, worthy of trust, and dependable. The word *"pistos"* comes from a related word, *"peitho"* that means *"settled persuasion."* That is the kind of person you want to pour your life into and that you want to have as the recipient of your legacy. You should focus on people of settled persuasion.

This settled persuasion is key to effective discipleship. We hear much these days about discipling and the discipleship process. Jesus told us to *"Go, therefore, and make disciples of all nations, baptizing them in the name of the Father and of the Son and of the Holy Spirit, teaching them to [obey] everything I have commanded you."* (Matthew 28:19-20) The key to effective discipleship is not teaching your disciples everything, but through teaching and by example bringing them to a point that they are willing to *"obey"* everything that is taught in Scripture. Biblical disciples do not know everything, but they are people of *"settled persuasion"* who willingly obey everything they know that is revealed in Scripture.

Examples of Legacy

One of the greatest joys of my life has been to live long enough to see second generation believers in Africa who are the fruits of my ministry during our missionary days, now themselves becoming faithful and fruitful multipliers. Last year I received a letter from one of our national pastor/leaders in Zimbabwe, and his words blessed my heart tremendously. He wrote in part, *"We are excited about this year's silver jubilee celebration of your legacy of evangelism in Tongaland out of which our faith and the faith of thousands of other Tonga men and women, young and old, has been born. This year we now have trainee pastors in all of the 40+ churches planted since the advent of your church planting mission, with the first baptist church planted in the Zambezi River Valley at Saba in 1992."* "Faithful men"—the key to a life of legacy!

On the top shelf of the bookcase in my office there are four hand-carved wooden eagles. They are posed as if perching in a high tamarind tree on the bank of the Zambezi. Two are facing away from each other, and two are facing as if looking into each other's eyes. The Zambezi River Valley Baptist Association presented those to me as a gift a few years ago on the occasion of the celebration of our 20th anniversary of work in the valley. As they presented them to me the spokesman said, *"Before you came to Africa we were like the two eagles that are facing away from each other. Our hearts were lost and we were going in our own way away from God. Since you came, our lives have turned around. Now we face God with hearts open and yielded. We gaze into His face with joy and we follow Him wherever He would have us to go. This is the legacy of your life among the Tongas."* Lives facing God with settled persuasion! That is the key to a Biblical pattern of discipleship and to leaving a legacy.

FAT People

On Friday morning, March 2, 2018, I sat watching on television the memorial service for one of the greatest evangelists in the history of the Christian faith. Billy Graham went to be with the Lord on February 21–arguably the most famous and successful preacher of the gospel in the history of the Christian church. Each of Billy Graham's children shared a word during the service honoring their father and his Lord and Savior Jesus Christ. Ned is the youngest child and youngest son. He made mention of the fact that each child had been given 3 minutes to speak and that since some of them had taken more time, he would take less. He chose to use a simple and often used acrostic to describe his dad. He described him as a FAT man. When it comes to leaving a legacy, FAT is a much popularized acrostic for the kind of people that we should look for and that we should pour our lives into. This acrostic, of course, has absolutely nothing to do with physical weight, body size, or eating habits. FAT is an acrostic that stands for Faithful, Available, and Teachable people. These are the kind of people you and I should spend our time pouring our lives into. These are the kinds of people who are those worthy of being objects of our legacy.

FAT people are first of all: 1) Faithful – That means they are reliable and loyal. They are people who can be trusted and depended on. 2) Available means that they have time to be discipled or mentored. The fact is, some people, as sincere as they may be, are just too busy with other things. My observation has been that a majority of professed believers neither have time to be mentored nor do they have time to mentor others in the depth of the faith. Usually their busyness is a matter of wrong priorities, their disinterest or inability to grow in the things of God; neither are they interested in mentoring others. They may indicate an interest in God's work and purpose, but the fact remains, they can only do so much until they get their priorities straight and get through that phase of misplaced priorities. You can only be effective at passing on your legacy with those who have time for the Christian life and who are willing to make God and His purpose the priority of life. These days, instead of mentors "discipling" mentees, peers are attempting to "disciple" peers and the shallowness of Facebook lowest common denominator theology is becoming the norm. 3) Teachable means that these are trainable people. Paul says that these men must be able to teach others also. No one is able to teach well unless he or she also is teachable. If Timothy had not been willing to receive teaching from Paul, he would not have been qualified to teach others also. A know-it-all, stubborn, self-willed man who wants to argue incessantly, or a person already stuck in a theological or traditional pattern will not be teachable. Being teachable means being willing to change your views when you become convinced from Scripture that you are in error.

The Thunder Poet

Watching the Light Come On

"And what you have heard from me in the presence of many witnesses, commit to faithful men who will be able to teach others also" (2 Timothy 2:2). It has been a thrill over the years to see the "light come on" in the hearts of young believers when faithful young men have come to realize that the missionary call of God is on their lives just like it is in the life of every other believer.

One of my most memorable church planting experiences was in an isolated village of Nanjili, Zambia. I shared previously in chapter 4 that Nanjili was one of the most responsive and spiritually hungry places I ever visited in the Zambezi Valley. One day I was teaching in that place about how God's Word tells us that each of us is called to be a missionary to the world with the gospel of reconciliation. On that particular day I had a group of volunteers with me who had come out from the states to spend a week or two with us there in the bush of the Zambezi River Valley. After I had taught a while, I stopped and asked a rhetorical question to the group of new believers who had gathered. *"How many missionaries are here today?"* A young man named Bautu, with quick wit and sparkling, intelligent eyes quickly lifted his hand and replied, *"One, and you are him."* I said, *"No Bautu. That is not the right answer."* Undaunted he lifted his hand once again and said, *"Then there must be four—you and these three guests visiting from the USA."* Once again, I said, *"No Bautu, you still aren't grasping the truth of what I have been teaching."*

After a while I paused in my teaching and once again asked the question, *"How many missionaries are present here today?"* A big smile came across Bautu's face as he lifted his hand and then said, *"TOONSE!" "We all are!"* I said, *"Yes, Bautu. That's the truth I've been wanting you to grasp."* Faithful men are men who can be trusted as reliable to maintain the standard of sound doctrine and who can be counted on to be dependable in fulfilling the ministry that has been entrusted to them.

These faithful men are the kind that you want to spend your time pouring your life into—the kind who *"will be able to teach others also."* This reduplication of disciples insures that your legacy continues to spread. If those you teach will teach others who in turn teach others, you're engaging in a ministry of multiplication. It may be slow at first, but the ministry ultimately can spread to hundreds, even thousands as it has been done in the Zambezi River Valley among the Tonga people.

Able

An essential thing to remember when it comes to the legacy process is that those who teach must be *"able."* That word *"able"* is translated from the Greek word, *"hikanos"* from the root "hik" = *"to reach"* or *"to attain,"* and it refers to that which reaches or arrives at a certain standard. In the context of 2 Timothy 2:2 it refers to able men who meet the standard and are fit, qualified, and able to teach.

The Thunder Poet

The reason you must pour your life into the lives of people who are *"able"* to then, in turn, pour their lives into the lives of others is that if you teach someone and he just bottles up the truth and doesn't pass it on, the process stalls out right there. Multiplication means reproduction becomes exponential growth in God's kingdom.

The primary meaning of *hikanos* is *"sufficient."* Interestingly, in the book of Ruth the Septuagint translators actually selected *"hikanos"* to translate God's Name, *"the Almighty." "The Almighty"* in that case literally means "the Adequate One," "the Sufficient One." He is *"adequate"* and *"sufficient"* and even more so for every need.

"And what you have heard from me in the presence of many witnesses, commit to faithful men who will be able [sufficient] to teach others also" (2 Timothy 2:2). When you are gone from this world, will there be a log left burning in the campfire? Pour your life into *"sufficient"* people.

Future Generations

"The character of our children tomorrow depends on what we put in their hearts today. If we expect the younger generation to grow spiritually, those of us who are older must pass on what we possess."[11] All believers have the responsibility to be sure that during their lifetime they have done something that has eternal ramifications that allows their legacy to live on into the next generation. Every one of us is like a link in a chain. There is a legacy left from a generation behind us which we inherited. There is a generation in front of us who is going to inherit what we leave.

Lavender Snow

Jacaranda trees are found all over Zimbabwe's towns and cities, lining the streets and sidewalks of some of the most beautiful suburbs in the country. They are even scattered across the countryside, and are occasionally found standing along river beds or on hillsides. I always look forward to their blossom. They are one of the most beautiful blossoming trees in the world with gorgeous lavender blossoms providing an enchanting shade of color.

The blooming of the Jacarandas also marks a change of seasons. They always bloom at the end of the dry "winter" and the blooming promises the hope that "summer" rains are coming soon.

Interestingly, in spite of its identification with the Zimbabwean countryside, the Jacaranda isn't Zimbabwean. It's an invader. The Jacaranda is in fact a "native" of South America, in particular of Brazil. The story goes that the plant was first introduced in 1899 to Fort Salisbury, the future Harare, capital of Zimbabwe, by a honeymooning couple who carried home six seedlings from a nursery in Durban, South Africa. Jacaranda trees soon took root in Zimbabwe's parks, gardens and alongside its road network.

Stunning lavender blossoms bloom on the limbs of the Jacaranda, but when the blooms die, they fall to the ground creating a beautiful purple carpet of

The Thunder Poet

padded petals. With the death of these blossoms they turn a drab lane into a dazzling pathway of lavender snow—one of the most spectacular sights in Africa. Thus, one of the most beautiful contributions of the Jacaranda comes from what they leave behind. That is so like the poetic legacy of the faithful believer.

Legacy—Life's Final Ministry Focus

The years are passing quickly now. I have become convinced that leaving a legacy is the final work of my lifetime. I want to be certain that I leave something that will outlast my presence and outlive my years. This legacy is important not only for those young men in Africa, but also for my own children, and my young associate pastors, and all of those who come after me who may be influenced in some way by my life and ministry. Are you leaving a legacy? Are you leaving something behind that will outlast your lifetime?

Shared Fire

I began this chapter by quoting a Tonga proverb. *"Mweenzu usiya chisisi."*—*"When a visitor departs, he leaves a log burning in the campfire."* This proverb speaks figuratively of the influence that our lives have on the lives of others. While the proverb relates figurative language, it represents literal truth as well. For example, it has occurred to me that many of the campfires built in Africa have their origin in "shared fire." By that I mean since matches are not always available in the bush, one of the ways fires are kindled at a new campsite is by borrowing fire from a local village. I have personally done this often. Many times my campfires were not started with the fresh flame of a new box of matches, but rather with borrowed coals from a neighboring cooking fire. In turn, whenever word got out of my impending departure from the area where I had been camping and from my campsite during those days in the bush, sometimes a young boy or young girl from a nearby village would come to my camp carrying in his or her hand a flat piece of tree bark. The child would then scoop hot coals from my mopane fire and place them on the bark in order to transport those coals back to a village for the purpose of kindling a new fire there. From that fire, another neighboring village might also send one to borrow fire, and so it goes on and on. Though it is impossible to know for sure, it is entirely possible that there are fires burning in Africa today that were originally kindled by my hand and brought to life with my breath years ago as I traveled through that land. This sharing of fire is a picture of what should take place from the influence of our lives. Are you leaving a flaming legacy? Have you left a log burning in someone's campfire? Through "shared fire" the influence of our life is multiplied a thousand times over.

In 2001, we left the Zambezi Valley as permanent residents for the last time, and there was a sense of permanency in our departure. Though we had cumulatively lived as residents in Africa on and off for a total of 11 years, the course of our resident journey

The Thunder Poet

there had covered two decades beginning in 1981. Work permits and health issues had caused us to move in and out of Africa three times. Those years were some of the most meaningful for each of our children, and their lives were influenced forever because of them. Our family is close knit in our love for one another and much of that is because of the experiences we shared together in the African bush and because of the shared legacy of looking for creative ways to share the gospel with people who need to know Jesus. Each of our children is engaged in creative evangelism techniques today, each in his or her own way.

    As I have mentioned before, during the course of our years in Africa the Tonga people honored me by giving me a ChiTonga name—Musungwaazi Munsaka. And as I have said in another place, Musungwaazi means "the encourager." I was given that name because I encouraged the Tonga people with the Word of God. During those years I, in turn, gave a Tonga name to each of our family members. Shirley is called "Chisoti." A chisoti is the top point on the roof of a Tonga hut. I gave her that name to remind our children and myself that she is the pinnacle of our family cohesion and that as wife and mother she should maintain an elevated position in our family life. Purity, our first-born daughter is "Muzuzumina," and that is the Tonga word for "echo." Rye is "Nkwazi Ila Chavindi," and his name means "a fearless eagle that flies alone." McKelvey, our youngest daughter is "Insasi." "Insasi" is the name for those sparks that fly off of a fire at night, shooting through the air and swirling upward toward the sky. True to her name she has a passion for evangelism and she loves to share her faith with others.

McKelvey was the only one of our children still living at home in Africa when our final departure time came. Purity was married by that time and living with her husband who was pastoring a church in New Mexico, and Rye was in college. McKelvey had been working for weeks on a handwritten note that she planned to put into a bottle and cast into the Zambezi on the occasion of our departure. She had written out a list of gospel verses from Scripture, a simple plan of salvation, and a personal note of greeting. The note read, "Whoever finds this, I hope you will read these Bible verses and do what God says you must do to be saved. My family and I are leaving Africa tomorrow, but I will pray for you and I hope God's Word will change your life like He has changed mine."

On the morning of our last day living on the banks of the Zambezi, McKelvey and I walked down to the river bank and cast the bottle into the water. Of course there is no way of knowing what became of the bottle and the note. We can only speculate about the outcome. I hope someone found it, and I pray they found Christ as Savior and Lord through it. I like to think that is the way the story ends, but in all honestly, who knows? Perhaps after reading the note, someone took the paper that it was written on and used it as kindling to start a fire in a remote village way up the Zambezi River. Perhaps even tonight a child snuggles up close to a fire, bracing herself against the cool breeze blowing across Lake Kariba,

The Thunder Poet

and while warming herself by the heat of the flames she wonders about the change she has seen in her father's life since he read the mysterious note he found in the bottle and since he responded to its truth. As her father begins to speak, he tells a strange story of finding a bottle with a hand-written note in it, and the beautiful passages from God's Word, and good news about forgiveness, life change, and redemption. As the child gazes intently into the blue and red flames of the hot burning mopane fire, perhaps she wonders about the source of the note. "Who wrote it? What was her name? Does she know that when she departed, she left a log burning in an African campfire?"

Are you leaving a legacy? Are you living your life to leave something behind? Your life will never rhyme with God's indigenous design until you begin to live that way.

There is a brilliant young Australian poet named Erin Hanson who is wise beyond her years. Her words challenge us to examine the way that we live. *"Perish the thought that ash be ash and not the memory of an ember."* When you are gone, will what you leave behind be only ashes, or are you leaving a blazing, life-changing log burning in somebody's campfire?

Chapter 8

Finding Rhyme on the Other Side of Fear

"Everything you've ever wanted is on the other side of fear."
George Addair[1]

It was eight minutes after sunrise when the bow of the Zia Sun leapt upward like an Olympic breaststroker surging above his swim lane to gasp his lungs full of air. Ever a cheerful heart, Mapulanga grinned as the thrust of the engine lifted his seat higher on the front deck of the cruiser. Even in the dim dusky grey of the early morning hours his white teeth seemed to be competing with the flash of his eyes to see which would outshine the other. He glanced at me through the semi-dark and nodded his pleasured approval at the growing wake churning from the powerful 350 cubic inch engine at the stern of the boat. A small dinghy tied to the cruiser with a length of khaki rope was teetering on the wake like a new puppy trailing dutifully behind its master. It rode awkwardly on the crest like an unsure and ambivalent surfer, occasionally breaking over the top to the outside as if making an attempt to run away. I intentionally kept the dinghy tied there whenever traveling to villages located on tributaries too small to accommodate the draft of the bigger cruiser. It was my only hope for navigating the shallows in some of those more isolated places of the upper recesses of the Zambezi River.

As I pushed the throttle forward, the cruiser leveled to a plane and Mapulanga relaxed against the resistant pressure of a smile-enhancing wind-stream that formed around his neck. He reveled in the cool morning air of the Zambezi Valley, his frayed collar flapping like a tattered flag in an arctic wind storm. Mapulanga loved the Zambezi. He was born on its banks and he never left there for all of his life.

An African fish eagle perching in the canopy of a tall ebony tree let out its melodic cry, its piercing call heard even above the deafening drone of the engine. Like a colonial flute player playing a tune with the force of a full-boiling tea kettle, the lonesome distinctive cry has been correctly described by many as "the voice of Africa." For those who have heard it, the sound is unforgettable.

Below the eagle, a large tire-colored, tread-backed crocodile stretched to its full length preparing to bask on a jetty of sand in the rapidly increasing heat of the morning sun. Its gaping mouth sported an arsenal of 60 to 72 milk-white ivory daggers, displaying a toothy grin that would put Willem Dafoe to shame. Mapulanga looked my way once again,

The Thunder Poet

lifting his eyebrows and shaking his head slightly as he motioned toward the crocodile and glared at the constant danger poised just beyond the boundary of our floating fortress of fiber glassed security.

With another forward push of the throttle we were racing up the river—dashing forward, yet heading back in time. We were hastening in hotfoot fashion toward a land that never hurries, toward regions from an ancient past, to villages inhabited by people not driven by schedule, and toward lands populated by simplicity where things have not changed for a long long time.

A Night in a Shallow Grave

Though I hesitate to ever call a daily dose of adventure uneventful, the trip that day was basically "uneventful," and we arrived at our destination slightly past mid-morning. I regret that I cannot more accurately recall the details of our ministry schedule that day. The specifics of everyday dynamic undertakings have a way of running together after a while. I am thankful, at least, that I can recall that I allowed Mapalanga to baptize our new converts that day. He was a faithful helper, and it was his last opportunity. He never traveled upriver with me again. Daily adventure includes many daily risks and dangers. Mapulanga, age 26, did not live to see another year.

By mid-afternoon we boarded the boat to head back to Siavonga, and we began to prepare for a long trip back down river. A strange smell of fuel greeted us when we stepped on board. I kept a five gallon jerry can stored under the cockpit in the bow of the boat for the purpose of refueling the small 2 ½ horsepower motor now hanging on the back of the ten-foot dinghy. The jerry can had dislodged and had come loose from its securing fasteners. The result was that the fuel had now spilled out soaking into the carpet of the cruiser, and had created both a smelly and dangerous situation for our trip back home.

By the time we had traveled a mile or so I realized we would not be able to make the trip under those conditions. We were standing in a slush of an inch or so of gasoline soaked carpet, and the fumes were beginning to cause dizziness and nausea even with the ventilating effects of traveling with an open canopy. Besides that, there was the danger of fire. I knew we would have to make an alternative plan.

I decided to beach the boat in a cove of one of the many deserted islands in Lake Kariba with hopes of coming back for it later the next day after some of the fuel had evaporated. Mapulanga and I would take the dinghy and continue our journey. It was a great plan with the exception of one thing. All the fuel needed for refueling the dinghy along the way for the trip back to Siavonga had been spilled out in the cruiser, and I was not sure if the remaining modest amount of fuel in the small tank connected to the vertical shaft outboard motor would be enough to make it home.

We secured the cruiser on a sandy beach and launched the dinghy. Once again we continued our journey, this time at a much slower pace—full-throttle

The Thunder Poet

speed powered with the capacity of only two and a half horses.

After a couple of hours, we had not made nearly as much progress as I had hoped we would. I switched off the engine and took my mini-mag flashlight out of its holster at my side and shined it down into the fuel tank. We were almost out of fuel. It was time for another decision. I looked at Mapulanga and explained the situation. We would have to find a flat sandy island and try to hold up for the night. He reminded me that we had not planned to stay out all night and that we had not brought along any camping gear or supplies. I said, *"We'll have to do the best we can."*

As the sun sunk low in the west and the glassy surface of Kariba morphed into a liquid clone of the red-orange sky, Mapulanga and I dug what looked like a shallow grave in the sand on a narrow beach of one of the many lonely unnamed islands in Lake Kariba. We removed the small motor from the back of the boat and secured it along with the fuel tank in a stack of driftwood. We flipped the dinghy over to cover the shallow grave and built a small campfire near the boat using the overturned vessel as makeshift camp stools. After sharing a wholesome dinner of biltong and a large can of peaches, we let our fire go out and crawled under the dinghy for shelter. After covering our bodies with sand for protection from the mosquitoes and tsetse flies, lying shoulder to shoulder in the shallow grave, we settled in to spend a long night.

Just before midnight we heard the first hippos and the crocodiles coming from the water to join us on the island for feeding during the night. Hour after hour we pulled the seats of the dinghy as close as possible against our chests each time the crocodiles or hippos came near the boat. The sounds of the hippos are loud, their grunts and bellowing thunderous like the decibel severity of semi-truck jake brakes at close quarters, but it was the frightful sounds of the big crocs that were most terrifying throughout the night. Their growls and hissings are horrific and much like the sound effects used for the dinosaurs in *Jurassic Park*. I cannot say that I have ever slept in a shallow grave, but I have buried myself in one to survive on more than one occasion on Lake Kariba. In fact, that one night the only hope for life and survival was a shallow grave.

The Shallow Grave Principle

The "shallow grave principle" is a term I often use as a description of dying to self spiritually, and it is the key to surviving and thriving in spiritual life. H. G. Bosch said, "Discipleship means crucifying the ego and putting Christ and others first."[2] Life never rhymes with God's indigenous design until life is fully surrendered to Him.

Jesus gave us the principle in John 12:24-26. He tells us there, *"I assure you: Unless a grain of wheat falls to the ground and dies, it remains by itself. But if it dies, it produces a large crop. The one who loves his life will lose it, and the one who hates*

The Thunder Poet

his life in this world will keep it for eternal life. If anyone serves Me, he must follow Me. Where I am, there My servant also will be. If anyone serves Me, the Father will honor him." According to Jesus the "shallow grave principle" leads to a full and fruitful life. The surrendered life that is given up freely to God, His will, and His ways is the life that rhymes with God's indigenous design. The essence of this rhyme is expressed in Jesus' words, *"Where I am, there My servant also will be."* Jesus described the servant as one who *wanted to be where Jesus is*. Jesus is not describing a forced slavery where the servant wants to be free from the master. He is describing a chosen, willing servant who desperately wants to be close to his Master.

The word our Lord uses to describe the *"servant"* in this passage is significant for our understanding. It is the Greek word *"diakonos." "Diakonos'* is a reference to a servant *'in attendance,'* one who is nearby the One being served. It is a reference to an intimately close personal servant. There is another word for "servant" used in Scripture. The word often used is *"doulas."* A *doulos* is a "bond-slave" and represents a servant who may serve at a distance: hence we understand the appropriateness of *diakonos* in this verse.[3] Jesus is not addressing a distant servant here. He is addressing a servant of intimate self-renunciation. He is challenging you to let go of you.

Watchman Nee wisely said, "Our spirit is released according to the degree of our brokenness. The one who has accepted the most discipline is the one who can best serve. The more one is broken, the more sensitive he is. The more we desire to save ourselves, in that very thing we become spiritually useless. Whenever we preserve and excuse ourselves, at that point we are deprived of spiritual sensitivity and supply. Let no one imagine he can be effective and disregard this basic principle."[4] Ego must be crucified if we are going to discover God's plan for a full and meaningful life. That burial in a shallow grave of crucified ego is the key to rhyming life with God's indigenous design.

A Follow-up Question

In a previous chapter, I asked what I described as a life-changing question—"What is the most important life response ever revealed in Scripture?" I pointed out that Jesus didn't leave us guessing. It is this: *"Love the Lord your God with all your heart, with all your soul, with all your mind, and with all your strength"* (Mark 12:30). Jesus taught us that nothing matters more than that. That's the number one thing in life. He is telling us, *"I want you to love Me passionately."* Nothing else matters in life if you don't love God passionately. God doesn't want you to love Him half-heartedly. He wants all your heart, all your soul, all your mind, and all your strength. That's what it means to be intimate in your relationship with God.

Here, though, is an important follow up question: If loving God with all your heart, all your soul, all your mind, and all your strength is the

The Thunder Poet

definition of intimacy in a person's relationship with God, how does a person grow in his intimacy with God? The simple answer is—growth comes in dying to self. Unfortunately many people believe intimacy comes from reading more Scripture, praying more, attending another Bible study, attending church more often, or getting actively involved in ministry. While all of those things are important and are generally indicators of spiritual growth, they are not where spiritual growth begins. Dying to self is the key. If you want to grow close to Christ you must die to self. Real life begins with a shallow grave.

Life Begins by Letting Go

The story is told of a pirate who was once returning home from a far journey spent raiding and plundering. He had spent many years lying, stealing, and cheating in a faraway land, storing up a great chest of treasure for himself. The pirate held on tightly to that chest because he saw in it something of much more value than just jewels and gold. He saw in that chest the fulfillment of all his dreams, hopes, and aspirations—what that treasure could buy and bring to his life. He thought that the treasure was his key to the future and to the "good life."

The pirate, having made his fortune, decided it was time to return home. He boarded a ship and began his journey home. While he was traveling, a storm arose, and it did not take long for the storm to overtake the ship. Soon the ship began to break into pieces, and eventually the pirate and his treasure plunged into the cold sea. Because he was desperately holding onto the treasure chest, he rapidly sank to the bottom. As the pirate was sinking, he had only one thought, "How can I get my treasure to the surface?" It was then that the pirate began to realize that life was not in the chest, at all. Life was on the surface, but holding onto the chest would cause him to die. Reluctantly the pirate let go of that chest and began to swim upwards toward the surface.5

What is the moral of that story? We are a lot like the pirate. We hold onto our agendas, our egos, and our fleshly desires, thinking all the while that these things will bring us life. In reality, they are pulling us down toward death. Jesus taught us, *"Don't collect for yourselves treasures on earth, where moth and rust destroy and where thieves break in and steal. But collect for yourselves treasures in heaven, where neither moth nor rust destroys, and where thieves don't break in and steal. For where your treasure is, there your heart will be also"* (Matthew 6:19-21).

Do you want to grow in intimacy with God? It begins with dying to oneself. Life always begins with a shallow grave.

"The Formula of Focused Attention"

Verse 24 of John 12 gives us a "heads up" about what is most significant. The Greeks have come to seek out Jesus' truth, questioning Him to understand the success of His ministry. Jesus responds by saying, *"I assure you . . . ."* Some translations begin, *"Truly,*

The Thunder Poet

truly . . ." These words essentially means, *"Wake up! Don't miss this! Think carefully about this because it's important! You can take this to the bank!"* Jesus always begins His teaching with these emphatic words when He is about to say something extremely profound. One pastor described these words as "the formula of focused attention."[6] Whenever we see these words, it means that we should pay close attention to what follows. With His analogy of a seed that must fall to the ground and die in order to produce a great crop, Jesus is saying real life doesn't come from pampering yourself, pleasing yourself, or putting yourself first. Real life comes from dying to self.

The Pattern of the Cross

"I assure you: Unless a grain of wheat falls to the ground and dies, it remains by itself. But if it dies, it produces a large crop. The one who loves his life will lose it, and the one who hates his life in this world will keep it for eternal life. If anyone serves Me, he must follow Me. Where I am, there My servant also will be. If anyone serves Me, the Father will honor him" (John 12:24-26).

Jesus is talking about Himself. He is the grain of wheat. As He speaks these words He realizes that unless He is willing to die, unless He goes to the cross, which He sees looming in the immediate foreground now, His whole purpose in coming to earth will have been wasted. He will remain alone. *"But if it dies, it bears much fruit."* He sees these Greeks as the first fruits, the symbol of a great harvest of Gentiles throughout the earth.

During His short ministry on earth, Jesus was constantly dying to Himself as He loved others. We see a graphic example of that in John 13, where Jesus took a towel and a basin of water to wash the disciples' feet. That was the job of a servant. But Jesus did it as an example of how we are to be willing to die daily to ourselves. Jesus Himself was the pattern for His teaching.

If the gospel that you hear preached on the radio, the television, or wherever, does not begin with a cross, or does not begin by telling you that something in you has to die, it is not the true gospel. The cross is the identifying mark. These words of Jesus radically cut across the philosophy of life today! Every television program, every magazine, and every popular song all present the philosophy, "Your life is your own! Live it the way you please! Watch out for No. 1! Do your own thing!"

If you are being told that the way to gain a deep and wonderful sense of self-esteem and a full and meaningful life is to simply come to Jesus with the intent of letting Him build up your own plans, expand your own agenda, and make you feel good about yourself, you are not hearing the true gospel of Jesus Christ. Life that rhymes with God's indigenous design does not begin that way. It always starts with a cross. The genuine life that God ordains for each individual does not begin with immersion into a comfortable recliner. It begins with burial in a shallow grave. It begins with death to self!

The Thunder Poet

Death to Self is the Beginning of the Gospel

Dr. A. W. Tozer, one of the great preachers of a few decades ago and a man who has deeply influenced my passion for the things of God, once defined the centrality and meaning of the cross as follows:

The cross is the symbol of death. It stands for the abrupt, violent end of a human being. The man in Roman times who took up his cross and started down the road had already said goodbye to his friends. He was not coming back. He was not going out to have his life redirected. He was going out to have it ended. The cross made no compromise, modified nothing, spared nothing. It slew all of the man completely and for good. It did not try to keep on good terms with its victim. It struck swift and hard and when it had finished its work the man was no more. That evangelism which draws friendly parallels between the ways of God and the ways of man is false to the Bible and cruel to the soul of the hearers. The faith of Christ does not parallel the world. It intersects it. In coming to Christ we do not bring our life up on to a higher plane. We leave it at a cross. The grain of wheat must fall into the ground and die. That is the beginning of the gospel.[7]

A Call to Die

Dietrich Bonhoeffer is a mystery. To say he was brilliant would be an understatement. He graduated summa cum laude from the University of Berlin in 1927 with a doctorate in theology, a stunning feat, considering he was only 21 years old. He taught seminary in the USA and Germany and pastored churches in London and Berlin. His writings are considered classics and many are required reading in some seminaries even today. He was arrested by the Nazis for his association and assistance with those involved in Operation Valkerie—a plot to assassinate Adolf Hitler. While in prison he continued to write and to teach. He was executed a mere three weeks before Berlin was liberated. Though he wrote many things, he is primarily revered for writing one book entitled, THE COST OF DISCIPLESHIP, and especially for one sentence in that book—*"When Christ calls a man, he bids him come and die."*

Bonhoeffer's association with liberal theologians later in his life and questionable theological statements he made in his latter writings have caused many to question his consistency. Because I personally find him to be a mysterious conundrum, I can't endorse his orthodoxy without question, but what he said in that one book is one of the finest statements on dying to self ever written. He said:

The cross is laid on every Christian. The first Christ-suffering which every man must experience is the call

The Thunder Poet

> *to abandon the attachments of this world. It is that dying of the old man which is the result of his encounter with Christ. As we embark upon discipleship, we surrender ourselves to Christ in union with his death—we give over our lives to death. Thus it begins; the cross is not the terrible end to an otherwise god-fearing and happy life, but it meets us at the beginning of our communion with Christ. When Christ calls a man, he bids him come and die. It may be a death like that of the first disciples who had to leave home and work to follow him, or it may be a death like Luther's, who had to leave the monastery and go out into the world. But it is the same death every time—death in Jesus Christ, the death of the old man at his call."*[8]

The call of Christ to die to self was a shock to the Greeks. Self-centeredness and self-enjoyment were at the center of life for them. For them these values were the chief good of human life, the supreme aim, the ruling direction of their whole world. So in calling them to substitute self-renunciation for self-culture, and self-sacrifice for self-gratification, the Lord Jesus was virtually asking them to reverse the whole direction and totality of their thought and conduct.

Nothing Kept Back

Death to self is the pattern for a life that rhymes with the indigenous design of God. In verse 25 of John 12, Jesus gives us a prescription for how we can find that kind of life. *"The one who loves his life will lose it, and the one who hates his life in this world will keep it for eternal life."* C.S. Lewis in his book, MERE CHRISTIANITY nails it:

> *The principle runs through all life from top to bottom. Give up your self, and you will find your real self. Lose your life and you will save it. Submit to death, death of your ambitions and favorite wishes every day and death of your whole body in the end: submit with every fibre of your being, and you will find eternal life. Keep back nothing. Nothing that you have not given away will ever be really yours. Nothing in you that has not died will ever be raised from the dead. Look for yourself, and you will find in the long run only hatred, loneliness, despair, rage, ruin, and decay. But look for Christ and you will find Him, and with Him everything else thrown in.*[9]

To *"hate"* our lives (John 12:25) is the same thing as *"denying ourselves and taking up our cross daily to follow Jesus"* (Luke 9:23). It means that we must daily repudiate a self-centered life.

The Thunder Poet

Lessons from a Shipwreck

There is a story in the 27th chapter of the book of Acts that beautifully illustrates this concept of letting go and dying to self. It is a story of shipwreck and adventure on the high seas as experienced in the life of the Apostle Paul. Paul and his companions were prisoners on a Roman ship, and they were sailing to Italy when a terrible storm arose. The ship was in danger of sinking at sea. The Bible tells us that there were 276 men on board. The ship was taking such a pounding that the crew decided to lighten the load then run the boat aground in a desperate effort to save the lives of the passengers and crew. In the final verses of the chapter, the men on board the ship took several steps to save the ship's inhabitants. These actions are analogous of steps that we must take in the process of dying to self.

Cutting Away Lifeboats

For example in verse 32 we read, *"Then the soldiers cut the ropes holding the skiff* [life boat] *and let it fall away."* In the process of dying to self and fully committing to Christ, we must be willing to cut away our securities—we must cut away the lifeboats. What that means is that we must be willing to let go of some of our safety nets. We must cut away some of those things in which we find our guarantees. Paul Borthwick says, "If we aspire to live like Jesus, our lives should have an element of chosen hardship because we desire to grow in character and desire to identify with those less fortunate than ourselves."[10] What we should be thankful for is that we have the privilege to choose. Most of us have choices, and we can choose whether or not we want to simplify our lives. Borthwick goes on to say, "The essence of poverty is to be without choices."[11] There comes a time when we must choose to cut away the lifeboats. Scott Wesley Brown has a song about that. The song is entitled . . .

Things

Things upon the mantle, things on every shelf,
Things that others gave me, things I gave myself.
Things I've stored in boxes that don't mean much anymore,
Old magazines and memories behind the attic door.

Things on hooks and hangers, things on ropes and rings,
Things I guard that blind me to the pettiness of things.
Am I like the Rich Young Ruler, ruled by all I own?
If Jesus came and asked me, could I leave them all alone?

O Lord I look to heaven beyond the veil of time,
To gain eternal insight that nothing's really mine
And only ask for daily bread and all contentment brings
To find freedom as Your servant in the midst of all these things.

The Thunder Poet

For discarded in the junkyards and rusting in the rain
Lie things that took the finest years of lifetimes to obtain.
And whistling through these tombstones, the hollow breezes sing
A song of dreams surrendered to the tyranny of things.[12]

If you and I are going to die to self by following the pattern of Jesus for our lives—rhyming life with God's indigenous design, then we must recognize His prescription of surrender. That pattern begins by "*cutting away the life boats.*"

Casting off the Anchors

Verse 40 of Acts 27 begins, *"After casting off the anchors, they left them in the sea . . . ."* This may be one of the most difficult parts of dying to self. We must walk away from whatever holds us back. That's what an anchor does. It holds us back.

I've thought about the pull of anchors many times over the years. I vividly remember the day our family left in 1991 to go back to Africa after a time of stateside assignment. Upon our return to the field, we had to leave our oldest daughter Purity in the states for her college education. I'll never forget saying "goodbye" to our daughter at the airport and the intense pain of looking into those trusting eyes, realizing I was saying "goodbye" to her for the last time for a long time. My heart was breaking with the thought of leaving our daughter behind in order to pursue God's call on our lives. At that moment I realized that I was about to cut away an anchor that I would have rather never to have had to cut. But Jesus said, *"the person who loves son or daughter more than Me is not worthy of Me"* (Matthew 10:37 b). That moment was like death. It was death. It was death to self for the sake of following Jesus.

Removing Control and Surrendering Destiny

The final portion of verse 40 describes the next step in dying to self: *"at the same time loosening the ropes that held the rudders. Then they hoisted the foresail to the wind and headed for the beach."* The final step in dying to self is to take control off of our own lives and to surrender our destinies to the hand of God.

You see, a rudder is what steers the boat, and so the rudder represents control. There comes a time when we must take control off our own lives and surrender our destiny to the blessed gales of God's Holy Spirit. Only then can we arrive at where God wants us to be. It is when we arrive at the point of self-abandonment that the Spirit of God begins to guide us in the direction that He would have us to go. God has a wonderful indigenous design for your life, but your life will never rhyme with that design until you release your self-control and surrender life to Him. Annihilation of self and obliteration of ego is an essential step in rhyming life. As Novalis describes it,

The Thunder Poet

it involves "casting yourself at the footstool of God's throne".[13]

The Completed Poem

In verse 26 of John 12, Jesus stresses how the poem of our lives is supposed to look when it is completed. *"If anyone serves Me, he must follow Me. Where I am, there My servant also will be. If anyone serves Me, the Father will honor him."* The poem's completion begins with an overwhelming appetite—what I might even call a consuming desire, to be near Christ. *"Where I am, there My servant also will be."* Yet, for the passionate pursuer it is not enough to be near Him, we must become like Him if the rhyme is ever going to be complete.

Too many professed believers view the goal of the Christian life as getting help from God for living a self-chosen life instead of submitting themselves to becoming like Him. Just like a seed produces grain of its own kind, so in lives surrendered to Christ, He produces men like Himself. By His death we receive both inclination and ability to become sons of God. *"For Christ's love compels us, since we have reached this conclusion: If One died for all, then all died. And He died for all so that those who live should no longer live for themselves, but for the One who died for them and was raised"* (2 Corinthians 5:14-15). By His death Christ has effected an entrance for this law of self-surrender into human life, has exhibited it in a perfect form, and has won others to live as He lived.[14] The meaning of life that rhymes with God's indigenous design is described succinctly in Romans 8:29, *"For those He foreknew He also predestined to be conformed to the image of His Son, so that He would be the firstborn among many brothers."* That is the purpose of God's poem. That is the essence of a life that rhymes. In fact, it is the way that God honors His faithful followers—*"If anyone serves Me, the Father will honor him."* There is no greater honor for the believer than to reflect the image of Christ in this world.

Years ago when Shirley and I surrendered to the call of God for our lives and left our home and native land to go out to Africa as missionaries, we found a life full of meaning and purpose. However prior to our departure I distinctly recall that there were those who came to me asking, "Why would you want to throw your life away? Why would you want to leave family and friends and a well-established life as a successful pastor to go to a dark and lonely place where your life may be wasted?" When they asked that question Jesus words came to my mind, *"I assure you: Unless a grain of wheat falls to the ground and dies, it remains by itself. But if it dies, it produces a large crop. The one who loves his life will lose it, and the one who hates his life in this world will keep it for eternal life. If anyone serves Me, he must follow Me. Where I am, there My servant also will be. If anyone serves Me, the Father will honor him"* (John 12:24-26). Without a doubt, those years on the mission field in Africa were the most meaningful and significant years of our lives, as well as when and where we learned most significantly what it means to die to self.

The Thunder Poet

As I have mentioned elsewhere, every year I go back to the place where we spent those years, and I take with me a group of volunteers who see for themselves that beautiful land where the "dying" took place. Looking back across all those years of what now seems so long ago, I'm so grateful to God that we said "yes" to Him and "no" to ourselves. It was there and among those beautiful Tonga people that we discovered His indigenous design. Others thought we were going there to die, but it was there that we learned how to live.

What Prevents Significant Indigenous Living?

If significant God-intended life comes for us through dying to self, why is it that more of us don't discover significant indigenous living? What prevents us from letting go of our self-consuming ego with full abandonment and surrender to the purpose of God? The simple answer is fear. Spiritually dying to self is as fearful for many people as sacrificing one's life physically. Many seem to avoid it at all cost. And the cost is extreme! Because of the fear involved in dying to self, some people never find the fulfillment of a God-designed life. They live and die without discovering the purpose for which they were born. Refusal to get beyond fear of the unknown and a lack of trust that God has our best interest in mind have caused many people to never risk surrender. God wants to fulfill our greatest potential, but many never realize that potential because they refuse to submit. They never experience an indigenous life that rhymes with God's purpose because they never push through to the other side of fear. All the while, a life that rhymes with God's indigenous design waits on the other side.

Elephant Graveyards

The legendary elephant graveyards of ancient African folklore were places where older elephants instinctively went to die when they reached a certain age. Tradition has it that they would go there, far from the group, to breath their last all alone. The myth was popularized in films such as *Trader Horn* and MGM's *Tarzan* movies. More recently, the 1994 Disney animated film *The Lion King* promoted the idea once again. Humans have always loved a good treasure story, so in parts of Asia and Africa there are tales told of a mythical elephant graveyards where valuable ivory lies just waiting to be found. According to these fanciful stories, the elephant knows when the end is near. Rather than trying to stick with the herd and potentially slowing them down, the elephant heads for the elephant graveyard. There he not only dies in peace, but also his descendants easily locate and visit his remains in the days that follow.

During one of our Rock Cry Expeditions a few years ago, I booked a game drive for our group through one of the local safari lodges near Hwange National Park. I was delighted when the lodge manager let me know that our guide for the afternoon would be a Tonga man that they called Stephen. A Tonga game guide might not always be as witty and

The Thunder Poet

entertaining as a Shona guide, or as handsome and tall as a Matabele one; however one thing is for sure, when you get a Tonga guide you can be sure he will have intense knowledge of African wildlife and a great deal of down to earth practical wisdom to boot.

That afternoon as we traveled throughout the deep bush of the park, we saw lots of animals, and our Tonga guide Stephen shared many facts, insights, and trivia about various species of African game. Late in the afternoon we stopped near a dry waterhole in the middle of the Dete Vlei where elephants were standing and where Stephen began to talk about elephant graveyards.

He explained with the simple, plain, direct English phrases, *"Elephant graveyards are a myth. A long time ago people thought they were a reality and many treasure hunters spent their lives looking for ivory in these elephant graveyards. Sometimes people do find a place where lots of elephant remains from old elephants are all collected all in one spot, but people misunderstand why they are there. Some have wrongly concluded that the elephants have come to that one spot to die, but they are wrong. The truth is that the elephants have a much better sense of smell than humans. They can even smell water buried deep beneath the earth. Sometimes when old elephants are too old and too tired to keep up with the herd they will come to a place like this dry water hole we are watching today. They smell the water beneath the earth, and they assume that the water will be coming back soon. Often, however, it is a long time before the water returns. By the time the water does return, or by the time the elephants discover that it is not coming back, they are too tired to leave that place, so many elephants die, all in one place. People assume it is an elephant graveyard."* Stephen went on to explain the scene of death, but then concluded by saying something that I have remembered for a long time. *"People think that these elephants have come here to die. In truth they have come here seeking to live."*

When I heard Stephen's words, I thought to myself, *"That's exactly why I came to Africa in the first place."* I didn't come to Africa because I wanted to die. I came to Africa genuinely seeking to live—to live out God's call and purpose with a surrendered life. That is what Jesus is talking about in verses 24-26 of John 12. He is not focusing on how to die. He is emphasizing how we truly live. These verses are not primarily a word about death, they are a word about living. The paradox of genuine Christian experience is that rhyming life with God's indigenous design always includes a shallow grave, and it always comes to those who by "dying to self" push through to the other side of fear.

The Other Side of Fear

Among my earliest childhood memories are those of being a carefree and fearless type of kid who spent his days engaged in self-manufactured adventure. The streams and rivers and the forests and fields of northeast Alabama were my playground, and the wild birds and animals were my playmates. Since

The Thunder Poet

we had no close neighbors in the area where my family and I lived, I learned quickly to enjoy solitude and solitary exploration. Remote and isolated places were as natural to me as parks and skating rinks were for city kids, and I spent my days finding treasures in bird nests, empty tortoise shells, and deserted hornet nests. I transformed the high perched limbs of China Berry trees into the imaginary masts of pirate ships. I collected weeping willow branches and repurposed them into bullwhips, and I traveled down endless corn rows standing on nearby farm fields imagining them to be canyons filled with outlaw hideouts from the old west. Dry stalks from last year's crop made excellent Comanche war lances, and soft moist sandy soil packed tightly around my hand formed sturdy toad houses when my hand was carefully and slowly removed. I caught fireflies by the dozens and harnessed the magic of flight by tying Mom's sewing thread to the hind legs of June bugs, releasing them to soar while I held wonder in my hand by grasping the other end of the string. Every day was a new exploit and I lived each day to the fullest.

My dad was the pastor of a little country church, so we weren't wealthy people. Life was simple, but I was unsophisticated and content, pleased as punch just to be alive. On my first day of school I boarded a big yellow school bus and along with my two older sisters I made my way toward my first adventure of daily interacting with my peers. I recall tremendous excitement as I sat on the bus decked out in a new pair of jeans rolled up three cuffs at the bottom to allow for growth and new plaid flannel shirt that my mom had made with her own hands. Just before I had walked out the door of our house, my mom had stuffed a brand new pack of Luden's cherry cough drops into my shirt pocket and sent me on my way with a kiss. She had purchased the cough drops for just a few cents at McClellan's five and dime store in Gadsden, but they were my life's greatest treasure on that first day at school.

My first grade teacher's name was Ms. Anderson. She was the oldest of the three Anderson sisters, all who taught at the Gaston School and who all were distinguished and dignified older women. I'm not sure how old Ms. Anderson was. As a six-year-old boy, I estimated her age to be somewhere in the neighborhood of a hundred. Maybe it was her snow white hair with that incredible blue rinse that made her look so "ancient of days." (I had seen a similar look on Charlton Heston as he portrayed an aging Moses in Cecil B. De Mille's film *The Ten Commandments*. The film had premiered the year prior to my enrollment in the first grade. I was fascinated with that blue-white color. It was very popular when I was a child. Jean Harlow had made it fashionable with her appearance in the 1930 film, *Hell's Angels*. Queen Elizabeth also contributed to its popularity in the 1940s—probably more about blue-white hair than you wanted to know.) Ms. Anderson was a sweet-spirited lady with blue-white hair, and she always treated me with patience and kindness. She never knew about the humiliating devastation I experienced later that day—that meltdown of secret shame that shook me

The Thunder Poet

deeply and set me on a course that changed my life forever.

The morning of my first day at school was fascinating for me. We began by reading from our first-grade reader, FUN WITH DICK AND JANE. "See Dick run. See Jane run. See Spot run." (Spot was my favorite character.) After reading class, we did art for a while and though each of us drew our pictures in conjunction with the assignment, the exercise did not result in the discovery of any prodigious new talent. It degenerated quickly into an approval-craving comparative pursuit with each child turning to his neighbor in the shared desks, hesitantly asking about his drawing, *"Mine is not very good is it?"* We so desperately wanted to hear someone say, *"Yours is good!"* (We learned this approval-seeking game on our first day of school, and we never stopped playing it.)

Lunch was a pleasure. My mom had packed a brown paper bag with two of my favorite sandwiches—Kraft cream cheese and pineapple, and a half-dozen peanut butter crackers. She had given me a nickel so I could buy a carton of chocolate milk to drink with my lunch. With a gentle late-morning southern breeze blowing, my new first grade friend Tommy Thompson and I sat on a big rock under the shade of a leafy oak tree and shared our lunch as we talked about our favorite TV western heroes.

By 1:30 PM it was time for recess. Those were days before organized recreation during recess for first graders, and each child was free to play in any way he wanted. I was in the mood to climb some trees.

Taylor

Although I looked for Tommy Thompson, he had gotten a stomach ache after lunch, so I was left alone. Not to worry! I had experienced some of my greatest adventures alone. I began to explore. I decided to check out what was located behind the school and found out there were forests there at the edge of the school yard. Perhaps I could find a good tree to climb. I watched squirrels playing in the tree branches for a little while: then I noticed that a hill rolled off from the schoolyard downward toward a little stream. The stream wasn't big enough to be called a creek. In fact, we always called such streams, a branch. I walked along the branch for just a couple of minutes watching the green frogs jumping into the water. I came to a place where a rock jutted out from the hillside. I knew I had to be careful not to get my shoes wet, but I knew if I were cautious I could slide around the rock without stepping into the stream. That, I proceeded to do, carefully hugging the rock as I slid around, but I was not prepared for what I was about to see. There on the other side of the rock was the notorious Thacker gang. They were smoking, and I had walked right into where they were hiding out.

    The Thacker gang was a gang of brothers and their cousins who were talked about throughout the school as a gang of guys that everyone wanted to avoid. It was only my first day at school but during lunch Tommy Thompson had already warned me about them. They were a rough looking bunch ranging in age from grade 5 to grade 12. They were as frightening to me as any band of robbers and cutthroats I had ever seen on the TV westerns.

The Thunder Poet

I swallowed hard and noticed that my mouth had gone dry. The oldest Thacker boy looked right at me and said, *"You're not going to tell anybody are you?"* I said, *"No!"* as I slipped back around the rock asking myself, *"What would Roy Rogers do?"* I scrambled back up the hill and quickly made my way back to the school. I entered the school through the brick-lined breezeway that separated the classrooms from the lunchroom. *"Whew! Maybe here I'll be safe."*

I walked as fast as I could toward the door to the hallway leading to the classrooms, trying to avoid running so as not to draw attention to myself. A few more steps and I could blend into the safety of the crowd. Then I saw them. Silhouetted against the bright glare of the far end of the breezeway they stood with an ominous arrogance like the Clanton gang at the OK Corral. The three oldest Thackers were standing there. I took a step back looking over my shoulder as I peddled backwards. As I did so, I caught a glimpse of the other two Thacker boys coming up behind me. They had me surrounded and I was afraid—not afraid like the fear you feel going up the first incline of a rollercoaster at the county fair or even the fear you experience when you're being chased across the front yard by your best friend's dog. I was afraid with the paralyzing fear that sets your chest on fire and draws your mouth like a weird reaction to Novocain.

One of the bullies grabbed me by the collar and pushed me up against a brick wall that lined the breezeway. Another grabbed my pocket and ripped the Luden's from my shirt. Then the gang leader threatened me and said, *"We better never see you outside alone again. And if you tell anybody, we'll make you sorry that you ever came to this school."* They pushed me down to the ground and then turned to leave.

When I finally got up I ran to the door and stumbled back to my seat in the first grade classroom. My mind was in a daze. I heard nothing else Ms. Anderson had to say for the rest of that day, and I replayed what had just happened a thousand times over as mental flashbacks played the scene in my mind again and again.

I felt the intensity of a new emotion. I was ashamed. My dad was a pastor, but he was no pacifist. He was a trained soldier, a veteran of WWII. He had taught me not to fight unnecessarily, but to stand up for myself when needed. Even though there was little I could do given the situation that I faced that day, before class was over I had convinced myself that I had failed in the face of fear and that I was a confirmed and irreparable coward. I felt so alone, and I felt I could tell no one. Shame began to consume my life.

The next day when I arrived at school, my life had changed. I had lied to my parents about the torn shirt, and I lost the joy of innocence by hypocritically trying to hide my pain. Every move now was calculated—always hiding, always watching, rapidly forgetting my natural smile. When recess time came, I lined up at the back of the line as students were about to go outside. Instead of going out with the other children, I quietly slipped from that position into the

The Thunder Poet

coat closet where I hid until the recess period had been completed—a practice I repeated often over the course of the next two and a half years. I was afraid, I was alone, and I was ashamed. My life had taken a tragic turn. The wonder, the passion, the joy, and the adventure were all gone. Fear of dying had destroyed my enthusiasm and passion for living. If this was life, I desperately needed for it to change.

At the beginning of my third grade school year, one the greatest things that could happen to a kid happened to me. My third grade teacher was a godly woman by the name of Mrs. Ushry. She was faithful to the Lord, and she was a genuine personal witness. She began each day of class with a reading from the Word of God, and she often freely shared the gospel—an action, by the way, that was actually legal in that part of the world at that time. By the springtime of the next year I was under deep conviction regarding my personal relationship with Jesus Christ. In addition to hearing the gospel on a regular basis at public school (a different day for sure), I also heard the gospel presented each and every week at the church where my father faithfully proclaimed the Word. Shortly after my 9th birthday I was ready to make a commitment of my life to Christ. I told my dad about my desire to trust Christ and make an everlasting commitment of my life to Him. He shared with me from God's Word passages of truth like John 3:16 that says, *"For God loved the world in this way: He gave His One and Only Son, so that everyone who believes in Him will not perish but have eternal life."* And passages like John 1:12 that says, *"But to all who did receive Him, He gave them the right to be children of God, to those who believe in His name."*

In response to that truth, on the following Sunday after the conclusion of our Sunday morning worship service I walked from the church to our home which was located next-door to the church. Just as I stepped up on the corner of the porch, I stopped and prayed a prayer of full surrender and submissive faith. The miracle of salvation came into my heart.

That day my life was changed and I had a new perspective and a new basis for living, claiming the promises of God's Word as my own and turning my back on a life dominated by fear. I began to learn and memorize Scriptures like Joshua 1:9, *"Haven't I commanded you: be strong and courageous? Do not be afraid or discouraged, for the Lord your God is with you wherever you go."* And passages like Isaiah 43:1, *"Do not fear, for I have redeemed you; I have called you by your name; you are Mine,"* and Psalm 34:4, *"I sought the Lord, and He answered me and delivered me from all my fears."* These are words that changed my life.

When I returned to school, I was a different kid. I believed God's Word and determined on the basis of it that I would no longer be afraid. He set me on paths of adventure that I never imagined as a child. In fact, He gave me a shot at authentic adventure by calling me to serve Him, and by giving me an international missions ministry in Africa among an amazingly wild and magnificent people. Remarkably, my ministry there was focused on freeing *"those who were held in slavery all their lives by the <u>fear</u> of* *death"* (Hebrews 2:15, emphasis mine). He has a way of rhyming our weakness with His strength.

The realities of fear and courage have played a major role in my life and the direction of God's call for it. The struggles and trials I experienced in those early days of elementary school were transformed into necessary discipline that equipped me to face situations I would have never believed I could have faithfully endured. I stand amazed at how God in His wisdom took time to patiently prepare my heart for the ministry and the life He has given me by transforming a grade-school coat closet into a training facility for how to deal with fear. In that sense a grade-school coat closet can be much like a shallow grave in the bush. In those dark lonely places He taught me how to die to self and how to deal with fear—how to walk in cadence with His poetic plan.

I'm No Longer a Slave to Fear

We sing a song in our church that has spoken volumes to my heart and is one of those special songs I find myself singing often during my quiet time whenever I am praising God. It is the testimony of my life and I rejoice before God whenever we sing it. *"No Longer Slaves"* is a song by Bethel Music featuring Jonathan David & Melissa Helser and it was released on August 21, 2015 as Bethel Music's lead single from their seventh live album, *"We Will Not Be Shaken."* The song won the "Worship Song of the Year" award at the 47th Annual GMA Dove Awards in 2016, with

Taylor

Jonathan David and Melissa Helser performing it at the ceremony.

> You unravel me, with a melody, You surround me with a song
> Of deliverance, from my enemies, Till all my fears are gone
> I'm no longer a slave to fear, I am a child of God
> I'm no longer a slave to fear, I am a child of God
>
> From my mother's womb, You have chosen me
> Love has called my name, I've been born again, into a family
> Your blood flows through my veins,
> I'm no longer a slave to fear, I am a child of God,
> I'm no longer a slave to fear, I am a child of God
> I'm no longer a slave to fear, I am a child of God
> I'm no longer a slave to fear, I am a child of God
>
> I am surrounded, By the arms of the father
> I am surrounded, By songs of deliverance
> We've been liberated, From our bondage
> Were the sons and the daughters, Let us sing our freedom
>
> You split the sea, So I could walk right through it
> My fears were drowned in perfect love
> You rescued me, And I will stand and sing
> I am the child of God
> I'm no longer a slave to fear
> I am a child of God
> I'm no longer a slave to fear
> I am a child of God.[15]

The Thunder Poet

When the Thunder Poet pens His poem, He writes no incomplete stanzas even when the verses appear gnarled and disfigured by fear. He writes no crooked lines even when the words seem twisting and curved on the pages of our apprehensive minds. He taught me that everything I ever wanted was waiting for me on the other side of fear.

Before the creation ever began, the God of all creation (that creation itself being the six stanzas of the primal poem of His innate design) wrote another poem, a pensive, personal, passionate poem that He by His great mercy decided to call by my name—a life-fulfilling particular poem designed just for me—one with which He graciously included me in the complete collection of His exhaustive works of poetic grace. It all began with a surrendered life and a divinely directed demise. By grasping that path of surrender, and through coming to grips with the extinction of self-worship, I found a life that rhymes with God's indigenous design.

The rhyme awaits you, too, you know—a poem of destiny written exclusively for you in the mind of God. <u>The Thunder Poet</u> has put your name on it. It is a life-changing, significance-impacting, fulfillment-producing, Christ-honoring rhyme written by the artistic hand of One Who is the King of song and rhythm. He yearns for a submitted heart and relinquished spirit, a life totally abandoned to Him. He longs for a heart that is fully devoted, a committed loyal soul that ardently pursues His will alone, a potential poem of His own making that willingly and wholly yields itself to His rhyme. It is time for you to discard your hiding place by deserting your coat closet, crawling from beneath your overturned dinghy, escaping your fortified ego by walking away from whatever form that self-manufactured fortress has taken for you. His masterpiece and your destiny are at stake. Do you feel a pull in your heart to become the refrain of His purpose? Will you respond by embracing the Thunder Poet's indigenous design?

The Thunder Poet

About the Author

Steve Taylor is a pastor, international missionary, adventurer, and author. For years he and his wife Shirley served as career missionaries in the Zambezi River Valley of Zimbabwe and Zambia where they worked among the remote River Tonga tribe. Steve currently serves as Lead Pastor of the First Southern Baptist Church in Pratt, Kansas. Each year under the name of Rock Cry Expeditions he leads a group of volunteers as they return to the Zambezi River Valley for a short-term, deep-bush mission trip. Throughout the year he travels extensively and is a much-in-demand speaker.

THE THUNDER POET—*Rhyming Life with God's Indigenous Design* is his second book. His previous book is an examination of spiritual warfare based 1 Peter 5:8-11 and is entitled, ALPHA PREDATOR—*How to Be Victorious over Life's Ultimate Adversary and What to Do When You're Not*. Steve's desire is to bring honor and acclaim to his Lord by writing about the greatness of God and amplified Christian living that results from a fully surrendered life. He writes with an extensive background of adventure and interaction with some of the wildest animals and locations in God's creation.

Among the traditional Bantu tribes of Southern Africa there are groups of official "praise-singers" who laud the tribal chiefs and kings. These individuals are called, "izimbongi" (Zulu) or "sikapeto" (ChiTonga). They live for the sole purpose of bringing esteem and commendation to the African monarchs. It is the privilege and duty of the "izimbongi" to walk before the king, leading his royal procession from the kraal. They salute and address him directly, referring to him through accolades that highlight his bravery, skills, greatness, and other positive attributes. These "singers" use images drawn from the local environment and from the universe to bring adoration to the sovereign.

Steve's purpose in writing THE THUNDER POET is to reduplicate the adoration and praise of the "sikapeto." His joy is to direct his praise to the great God of all creation.

NOTES

Introduction: A Life That Rhymes

[1] Blake, William. The Poetical Works of William Blake, ed. by John Sampson. (London, New York: Oxford University Press, 1908), Bartleby.com, 2011.

[2] Browning, Robert. *Paracelsus,* (London: Effingham Wilson, Royal Exchange, 1835) Page 71.

[3] https://vextmagazine.blogspot.com/2014/07/yevgeny-yevtushenko.html

[4] biblehub.com/commentaries/hastings/Ephesians/2-10.htm

[5] https://www.coursehero.com/file/p4qrjh4o/The-Greek-verb-ποιεω-poiéo-I-make-or-create-gave-rise-to-three-words- ποιητης/

[6] Tada, Joni Eareckson. A Place Of Healing: Wrestling With The Mysteries Of Suffering, Pain, And God's Sovereignty, (Colorado Springs, Colorado, 2010, David C. Cook) Page 67.

Chapter 1-Creation's Testament

[1] Christensen, Allan Conrad, <u>The Subverting Vision of Bulwer Lytton: Bicentenary Reflections,</u> (University of Delaware Press, 2004) Page 243.

[2] Marie Dacke et al. *Dung Beetles Use the Milky Way for Orientation.* "Current Biology", published online January 24, 2013; doi: 10.1016/j.cub.2012.12.034

[3] Herschel, William J. quoted in: Morris, H.M., <u>Men of Science, Men of God</u>, (El Cajon, CA, USA, Master Books, 1982) Page 42.

[4] <u>http://ngtt.journals.ac.za/pub/article/viewFile/7/6,</u> "The necessity of natural theology?" In conversation with John Calvin on the human senses, September, 2011, Page 68.

[5] *The Three Amigos*, Directed by John Landis (1986, Simi Valley, California, Coronado National Forest, Old Tucson Studis, and Hollywood, HBO Films and Orion Pictures)

[6] Mason, Mike, <u>The Gospel According to Job</u>, Chapter-"The First Gospel", (Wheaton, IL: Crossway Books, 1994) Page 144.

[7] <u>https://waitbutwhy.com/2013/11/4-mind-blowing-things-about-stars.html Tim Urban.</u>

The Thunder Poet

Chapter 2-The Voice of the Wilderness

[1] https://www.goodreads.com/quotes/29556-some-people-talk-to-animals-not-many-listen-though-that

[2] The Wilderness Act of 1964, Public Law 88-577(16 U.S.C. 1131-1136) 88th Congress, Second Session, September 3, 1964 (As amended) (Wilderness Connect, The University of Montana).

[3] http://www.sermonsforyou.co.uk/?q=node/38, "In the Wilderness".

[4] Stojanovic, Dejan, "Dancing of Sounds", http://americanpoems.weebly.com/dancing-of-sounds.html

[5] Newhall, Nancy, as quoted by John McPhee, Encounters with the Archdruid, (Farrar, Straus & Giroux, 1971)

[6] Carr, Alan, The Choosing of the Twelve, (Mark 3:13-19) Sermon Notebook.org

[7] https://en.wikipedia.org/wiki/Abe_Gubegna

[8] Bell, Brian. https://www.studylight.org/commentaries/cbb/2-corinthians-3.html

[9] Ogilvie, Lloyd John, When God First Thought of You, (Waco, Texas, Word Books, 1978) Pages 13-14.

[10] From Class Notes, Dr. Jack MacGorman, Professor of New Testament, Southwestern Baptist Theological Seminary, 1976.

Chapter 3-Snake Stories

[1] *Raiders of the Lost Ark,* Directed by Steven Spielberg. (1981, Yuma, Arizona, Tunisia, Hawaii, France, Paramount/Lucas Film)

[2] https://christiananswers.net/dictionary/serpentfiery.htm

[3] Pink, Arthur W., Exposition of the Gospel of John. (Zonderman, 1968)

[4] Quote from H. Thorne. https://biblehub.com/commentaries/hastings/numbers/21-8.htm.

[5] Pritchard, Ray, In the Shadow of the Cross: The Deeper Meaning of Calvary, (Nashville, Tn., Broadman & Holman, 2001)

[6] Thompson, Bert, Ph.D., *"Did Death Occur on Earth Prior to Man's Sin?"* http://www.apologeticspress.org/apcontent.aspx?category=11&article=677

The Thunder Poet

[7] http://www.trinityosceola.com/home/180012081/180012081/files/March%2015-%202015.pdf

[8] Benjamin, Jyothi, "The Bronze Serpent", Vol. 3 Issue 1, http://lutheranmissions.org/b-a-s-i-c-271/

[9] Aesklepius had a Sumerian, Counterpart, Things you don't learn in medical school: Caduceus. https://www.ncbi.nlm.nih.gov/pmc/articles/PMC4439707/ April, 2015

[10] https://www.livescience.com/43559-black-mamba.html

[11] Shen, Helen, "Deadly Snake Venom Delivers Pain Relief", Nature Journal, October, 2012 https://www.nature.com/news/deadly-snake-venom-delivers-pain-relief-1.11526

[12] "Land Reform in the Twenty Years After Independence," https://www.hrw.org/reports/2002/zimbabwe/ZimLand0302-02.htm

[13] https://en.wikipedia.org/wiki/Gukurahundi

Chapter 4-The Sapient Safari

[1] https://fyppsychology.com/post/130114488465/quotes-mihaly-csikszentmihalyi-goals-transform-a-random.

² Sorge, Bob, Secrets of the Secret Place: Keys to Igniting Your Personal Time with God., (Oasis House, 2012).

³ Rupiah, Martin R., "A Historical Study of Land-Mines In Zimbabwe, 1963-1995", (Zambezia, Volume 22, Issue 1, Jan. 1995) Pages 63-78.

⁴ Moule, Hadley C.G., Ephesian Studies: Expository Readings on the Epistle of Saint Paul to the Ephesians (New York: A.C. Armstrong and Son, 1900), Page 265.

⁵ Wuest, Kenneth S., Wuest's Word Studies from the Greek New Testament: For the ..., Volumes 1-3, (Wm. B. Eerdmans Publishing Company, Reprinted 2002).

⁶http://daddybstrong.blogspot.com/2009/10/wisdom-of-george-carlin-on-aging-enjoy.html.

⁷ Barber, Wayne Dr., "The Power Of The New Garment-Ephesians 5:6-14" http://preceptaustin.org.

⁸ Pritchard, Ray, "Redemption: Free at Last!", https://www.keepbelieving.com/sermon/1995-03-26-redemption-free-at-last/

⁹http://www.preceptaustin.org/index.php/redeem the_time, John Broadus quoted

The Thunder Poet

[10] Wayland, Francis, <u>A Memoir of the Life and Labors of the Rev. Adoniram Judson, D.D.</u>, (Boston: Phillips, Sampson, and Company. London: Nisbet and Company, 1853), Page 33.

Chapter 5-Plagiarized Poems and Passionless Lives

[1] Seuss, Dr., <u>Did I Ever Tell You How Lucky You Are?</u> (NY: Random House, 1973)

[2] <u>https://www.elephantsforever.co.za</u>

[3] McPherson, Miles, <u>God in the Mirror: Discovering Who You Were Created to Be</u> (Grand Rapids, Baker Books, 1982) Page 14.

[4] <u>https://www.nationalgeographic.com/photography/proof/2017/06/hummingbirds-slow-motion-flight-videos/</u>

[5] <u>http://hawkenscribe.blogspot.com/2013/12/we-are-same-yet-different-paradox-in.html</u>

[6] Ryle, J.C., <u>Practical Religion : Being Plain Papers on the Daily Duties, Experience, Dangers, and Privileges of Professing Christians</u> (London: William Hunt and Company, 1883)

7 https://www.goodreads.com/quotes/12747-wherever-you-are-be-all-there-live-to-the-hilt

8 Edwards, Jonathan, The Works of Jonathan Edwards, Volume 1: Freedom of the Will (The Works of Jonathan Edwards Series)

9 https://bible.org/seriespage/lesson-82-how-serve-lord-romans-1211

10 https://enewhope.org/sermon/notes.php?id=W1031

11 http://www.cjmahaney.com/blog/the-sluggard/

12 Harmon, Justin, "6 Reasons Why Your Comfort Zone Is Holding You Back In Life" (Blog) https://www.lifehack.org/articles/communication/6-reasons-why-your-comfort-zone-holding-you-back-life.html

13 https://adamkurihara.wordpress.com/2013/02/20/john-wesleys-directions-on-singing-1761-and-some-annotations/

Chapter 6-Nesting in a Shadow

1 https://www.goodreads.com/quotes/174867-poetry-is-an-echo-asking-a-shadow-to-dance

The Thunder Poet

[2] http://www.sundaynews.co.zw/lobengula-caves-abound-with-mysteries/

[3] Ellicott, Charles John. "Commentary on Psalms 91:1". Ellicott's Commentary for English Readers. https:https://www.studylight.org/commentaries/ebc/psalms-91.html. 1905

[4] Hester, Dennis J., The Vance Havner Quotebook, (Baker House Group, 1987)

[5] Forsyth, P.T., The Soul of Prayer, (Grand Rapids, Michigan, William B. Eerdmans Publishing Company, 1916)

[6] Darlow, T.H., The Upward Calling, (Jennings and Graham (1906), Page 38.

[7] Watson, George Douglas, *Others May-You Cannot* (Tract), (Christian Communicators Worldwide), www.CCWtoday.org

[8] McGee, J. Vernon, Thru the Bible Vol. 54: The Epistles (1 Peter), (Nashville, Tn. Thomas Nelson, Inc., 1981) Page 9.

[9] West, Robert M., How to Know God's Will: What the Bible Says, (Barbour Publishing, 2012) Page 12.

Chapter 7-A Log Left Burning in an African Campfire

[1] https://www.goodreads.com/quotes/7902060-the-irony-of-life-is-our-greatest-fear-is-to

[2] Barine, Stephen and Barine,Karimi, A Life Well Lived: Living to Leave a Legacy, (Integrity Publishers, Inc., 2009)

[3] *The Dead Poets Society*.Haft, Steven (Producer). Schulman, Tom (Director). (1989, Buena Vista Pictures Distribution)

[4] https://www.keepbelieving.com/articles/the-legacy/

[5] Jernigan, Carl, Images-quote It's the 'jump' or the 'bounce'

[6] O'Callaghan, Jonathan, "What is the Southern Cross?", https://www.spaceanswers.com/solar-system/is-it-possible-for-neptune-and-pluto-to-collide-given-that-their-orbits-cross/

[7] White, Ivery, Teaching With Purpose "Shaping the Kingdom, One Mind At a Time", (LuLu.com, 2013) Page

[8] https://www.goodreads.com/author/quotes/6497812.Ayesha_Siddiqi

[9] Byington, Teresa,"Key to Successful Mentoring Relationships", Tools of the Trade (Volume 48-Number 6-December, 2010) https://www.joe.org/joe/2010december/tt8.php

[10] "Our Mission is Clear: Train Others To Train Others",http://www.preceptaustin.org/2_timothy_21_-7 (Updated May, 2018)

Chapter 8-Finding Rhyme On The Other Side Of Fear

[1] Addair, George, Quote https://www.goodreads.com/quotes/1216350-everything-you-ve-ever-wanted-is-on-the-other-side-of

[2] Bosch, H.G., As quoted by Brian Bell in a sermon (John 12:12-26) Entitled, "Letting Go of You!", messages.calvarymurietta.com, July 12, 2009.

[3] Dods, Marcus, Expositor's Greek Testament (John 12:26), (Grand Rapids, Michigan: William B. Eerdmans Publishing Company, 1979)

[4] Nee, Watchman, "The Release of the Spirit", Sermon, http://www.peacemakers.net/unity/wnrelease.htm

[5] Nerreau, Christopher, "Dying to Self", https://www.sermoncentral.com/sermons/dying-to-

self-christopher-nerreau-sermon-on-political-freedom-117789

[6] Stedman, Ray C., God's Loving Word: Exploring the Gospel of John, (Discovery House, 2015)

[7] Tozer, A.W., Man the Dwelling Place of God, (Moody Publisher, 2008), Page 42

[8] Bonhoeffer, Dietrich, The Cost of Discipleship, (New York: Touchstone, reprint 1995)

[9] Lewis, C.S., Mere Christianity, (New York: HarperOne, 1952)

[10] Borthwick, Paul, How to Be a World-Class Christian: Becoming Part of God's Global Kingdom, (Westmont, Illinois: Press, 2012) Page 99.

[11] Borthwick, Paul, How to Be a World-Class Christian: Becoming Part of God's Global Kingdom, (Westmont, Illinois: Press, 2012) Page 98.

[12] Brown, Scott Wesley and Darin, Bobby, *Things* (Song)(Sparrow Records/Sparrow, 1995)

[13] The New Quarterly Review or Foreign, and Colonial Journal. Volume 7, April and July. London: John W. Parker, West Strand 1846. Page 168.

The Thunder Poet

[14] Dods, Marcus, <u>The Expositors Bible, The Gospel of St. John</u>, Volumes 1 & 2, (Woodstock, Ontario: Devoted Publishing, 2017) Page 132.

[15] Helser, Jonathan, Case, Joel, and Johnson, Brian, *No Longer Slaves* (Song), (Bethel Music, August 21, 2015)

The Thunder Poet

(Check out Steve's previous book here!)

Alpha Predator is an adventure-saturated exposition of 1 Peter 5:8–11, uniquely illustrated with stories of true-life encounters with African lions and memoirs from the author's life while living in the bush of Southern Africa. It is a book about conflict with Satan, defeat and failure in the believer's life, and the impact of the restorative grace of God. It is about hacking one's way through the overgrown jungles of hopelessness, exploring the massive floodplains of merciful forgiveness, and rejoicing on the vast open savannahs of deliverance. Alpha Predator is about the forfeiture and restoration of a cherished relationship with the Father. It is a literary safari into seldom explored regions of the heart of God and a candid excursion into the deepest longings of the heart of a banished child. For those who are desperately searching, this book holds the key to the way back home.

(Available on Amazon)

Taylor

The Thunder Poet

ALPHA PREDATOR (Sample)

INTRODUCTION The Tragic Death Of A Young Man In Africa

"Ah, Mufundisi, they only found small pieces of his body scattered through the bush!"

Mapulanga wasn't smiling as he related the story, and Mapulanga had the greatest smile I've ever seen on the face of an African. We were standing together under the shade of a lemon tree. I had been watching Mapulanga's melancholy expressions all morning, and I had seen the signs of sadness etched across his face, so I had not yet spoken. The African way is not to rush in the midst of emotion. Still, I genuinely wanted to know what had happened, so when I caught his glance, I asked him with my eyes. He began to tell the story.
"*It was there.*" he said, as he shook his head, lifting his chin and pointing with pursed lips to a place just across from our house on the Zambezi River. *"It was there where we see the light shining every night from those light globes powered by the big generator at that safari camp near Matusadona."*

Taylor

I reached up and pulled a lemon from the tree, stuck my thumb into it and peeled it back as I took a seat on a nearby rock. I used the peeling as a pointer to motion toward another rock as I offered Mapulanga a seat. He took his seat and spoke softly once again, *"This is the story they tell. It seems a young man had come out from England on holiday with a group of his friends. They were taking pictures of the animals there in the bush. When darkness came, they sat around the fire talking until they were tired. When the young man went to his bed where he had pitched his tent far from the others, he left the tent door open. When the night became quiet and still, the lions came looking for food. Everyone was awakened by the screaming. The lions took that young man from his tent and they ate him right there while the others were listening. Ah, Mufundisi, they only found small pieces of his body scattered through the bush!"*

Though brief and straight to the point – so typical of the way the BaTonga people narrate a story – Mapulanga's words left a haunting picture hanging in my mind. I found myself thinking often of the episode over the next several days. Having many times seen prides of hunting lions violently ravage their prey in the remote area of the Zambezi River Valley where my family and I were living as missionaries at the time, I could readily visualize how terrible the final moments of the young man's life must have been. When during the following week I finally made my way into town, the newspaper reports only verified what I had already begun to assume had taken place.

"I heard a horrendous yell!" The newspaper quoted David Boyle, a fellow photographic tourist, as he described

The Thunder Poet

the horrible death of the nineteen-year-old British student whose life-long dream it had been to spend a year in Africa. *"I didn't know if it was human or animal. But it was long and loud, and it was suddenly cut off, followed by the prolonged sound of growling."* [1]

I stood reading the description of how in the pre-dawn darkness of that ominous August night in 1999, David Pleydell-Bouverie was attacked and savaged by a pride of ten to twelve lions. According to the reports, he died only a minute or two after the attack began. But by that time, much of his body had been shredded and eaten by lions in the deep bush of the Matusadona wilderness area in Northwestern Zimbabwe. When the sun came up the next morning, local game rangers found parts of his dismembered body strewn through the bush up to twenty yards from his tent.

Unaware, We Had Been Watching from the Far Side of the River

On the night of the attack my family and I had been sitting on the front veranda of our home in Siavonga, Zambia, looking across the river, as we often did, gazing at the lights of Zimbabwe dancing on the surface of the water. We often entertained ourselves in the evening by imagining what life must be like for those people enjoying the adventure of falling in love with Africa for the first time in the safari camps there on the other side.

The red-orange light was the first to fade as the guides and tourists grew tired and let the camp fires burn low. Soon the brighter white lights also faded as the generator motors were switched off in the safari camps; their dying mechanical coughs sending alien sounds of false security ringing through the forests as the tourists made their way safely to their tents. Nobody ever dreamed that night the young Englishman would fail to heed the warning to keep his tent tightly zipped. Nor did they expect him to pitch his tent at a distance dangerously far from the main group. But neither did they expect him to be dead within the space of just a couple of hours of time from when they walked away from the fire, wishing one another a pleasant sleep.

The young man had spent such a wonderful day of game-viewing, sight-seeing, and photography with his friends. But life in the African bush is always uncertain and tenuous at best. The lions were roaming that night, looking for an easy meal, and young David Pleydell-Bouverie was selected as the target.

For the next several weeks, I found myself dwelling on the events surrounding the young man's death. After all, I personally had camped many times in the same general area – alone and unprotected except for the companionship of the faithful African people. The more I investigated the details of this tragic event, the more I discovered that David Pleydell-Bouverie had died for all the wrong reasons. Avoidable circumstances, mistakes, and human error all contributed to his untimely death.

A Terrible Reminder of the Words of Peter

The young man's death was a terrible and graphic real-life reminder of the words of Peter in 1 Peter 5:8-11. In these verses, Peter writes a warning about a horrendous Alpha Predator who is roaming the earth *"like a roaring lion"* seeking to destroy the lives, and annihilate the

The Thunder Poet

testimonies of God's people. *"Be sober! Be on the alert! Your adversary the Devil is prowling around like a roaring lion, looking for anyone he can devour. Resist him, firm in the faith, knowing that the same sufferings are being experienced by your brothers in the world. Now the God of all grace, who called you to His eternal glory in Christ Jesus, will personally restore, establish, strengthen and support you after you have suffered a little. To Him be the dominion, forever. Amen."*

Of all the followers of Christ living during New Testament times, Peter was uniquely qualified to issue this warning and impart this promise. He had personally fallen victim to the Alpha Predator's attack one night when he had repeatedly denied the Lord, even after he had convinced himself that he never would. He had known the dreadful pain this Adversary is capable of inspiring. He had become fully aware of how subjective failure can open the door to a full-scale attack by this awesome Pillager.

Perhaps that pain is the thing that makes it easy for so many of us to identify with Peter. He writes as a fellow struggler who has been through a very personal and violent encounter with the Alpha Predator. That encounter had resulted in defeat and failure, leaving him reeling in spiritual downfall and remorse. Had it not been for the grace-drenched initiative taken by the Lord to bring about Peter's restoration, he would have gone to his grave as a broken and defeated man.

The Anatomy of Restoration

This book is a book about defeat, failure, and restoration in the believer's life. In it I invite you to take an honest look at how to be victorious over life's ultimate adversary and what to do when you're not victorious. I really wish I could say I am writing *only* from a hypothetical perspective. I would like to be able to say that none of the references to failure and defeat found here have any basis in the historic reality of *my* life. But, honestly I have to tell you, that fantasy is not the case. I know what it is to fail and I know what it is to be defeated. I know what it is to be discouraged and to be knocked out of the race. I know what it is to have such a terrifyingly close face-to-face confrontation with the Alpha Predator that I have seen the reflection of myself deep in the orbs of those giant unblinking amber eyes. And gazing at that reflection, I know what it is to be ashamed – ashamed for not seeing in that reflection a likeness of the Lord, but rather the misshapen caricature of a wounded and broken man – a dishonorable contortion of the person He created me to be – a defeated and fallen facsimile of the intention of God for my life.

But thankfully, I also know what it is to be the unworthy recipient of a restorative work of grace – undeserved and unattainable apart from an acknowledgement of my helplessness, frailty, and absolute dependence on God. I know what it is to find release in the refuge of an honest heart before the Father, to learn the vernacular of confession and contrition, the one true dialect of deliverance that communicates the way back home.

The Thunder Poet

Thus I know what it is to enter a period of self-imposed seclusion, to find a lonely place where I could concentrate on re-establishing the vital connection of my heart with the only One in Whom I have ever found liberation. I know what it is to make enforced solitude and obligatory isolation the daily occupation of my life. I know what it is to sit day after day in the silent places of the night, and in the quiet places of the day, in obscurity and separateness with an open Bible on my knees, waiting and listening for the Voice of the Holy One in the pages of His Word.

I know what it is to find in those pages a God-designed soul-friend, a faithful *anamchara** of sorts with whom I could identify and who could instruct me through a passage in his first letter to an understanding of the anatomy of restoration. *(Anamchara* is a beautiful old Gaelic word and literally means *"friend of the soul."* It was originally used in the ancient Celtic churches to describe someone who shared another's jail cell as an encouraging companion and to whom one confessed, sharing the most confidential aspects of his life. Ray Simpson defined an *anamchara* as *"A soul friend who helps a person re-weave the scattered elements of his life into a new wholeness.")*[2] This picturesque passage from the Apostle Peter's writings (1 Peter 5:8-11) serves as the Scriptural basis for this book and as an outline of God's process of restoration in the believer's life. It is the description of the restoration of a real life of a real believer.

This restoration experience is too significant for me not to share! The reason for this is simple – sooner or later the Alpha Predator launches his attack on the life of every believer. Even if the believer doesn't fail in the midst of the attack, he often fails in his successive response to it. I have a feeling there are many people out there who need a word of hope from the personal experience of an actual life. They desperately need to hear the truth that according to God's Word, restoration after failure and defeat is not only conceivable and authentic, it is intended, expected, and made possible by God.

So, if today you find yourself in a fight for your life with life's ultimate Adversary, or if you have already been conquered in the fight and find yourself thinking because of your defeat, life for you has come to an end and your relationship with your Lord can never be what it was before, then this book is for you! While the Bible makes it clear there is an "Alpha Predator" who is real, cunning, and ferocious – a marauder who destroys, plunders and devours – the Bible also makes it clear there is One Who is both Alpha and Omega, infinitely greater than any Accuser, and <u>the final word is always His</u>. He holds the keys to forgiveness, restoration, and the rebuilding of your life! "<u>To Him</u> be the dominion forever! Amen."

www.ingramcontent.com/pod-product-compliance
Lightning Source LLC
LaVergne TN
LVHW041613070426
835507LV00008B/205